LAND SEA SHELTER CULTURE

AHL and a story of modern architecture in Hawai'i.

ORO
EDITIONS

Publishers of Architecture, Art, and Design
Gordon Goff: Publisher

www.oroeditions.com
info@oroeditions.com

Published by ORO Editions

Graphic Design: Middle Management
ORO Managing Editor: Kirby Anderson

10 9 8 7 6 5 4 3 2 1 First Edition

Library of Congress data available upon request. World Rights: Available

ISBN: 978-1-943532-33-9

Color Separations and Printing: ORO Editions, Inc.
Printed in China.

International Distribution: www.oroeditions.com/distribution

ORO Editions makes a continuous effort to minimize the overall carbon footprint of its publications. As part of this goal, ORO Editions, in association with Global ReLeaf, arranges to plant trees to replace those used in the manufacturing of the paper produced for its books. Global ReLeaf is an international campaign run by American Forests, one of the world's oldest nonprofit conservation organizations. Global ReLeaf is American Forests' education and action program that helps individuals, organizations, agencies, and corporations improve the local and global environment by planting and caring for trees.

Reflecting here from our 21st-century perch, it is with some wonder that I look upon Architects Hawaii Limited's impact over the past 75 years. At each decade, the buildings tell stories of the time, connecting our architecture to the land, its culture, and its future.

In a way, this book helps fill a void in the collective story of Modernism in America. From our own varieties of Critical Regionalism to the most successful evolutions of Brutalism, Hawai'i offers, much like our flora and fauna, unique species of design not found elsewhere in the world. We hope you enjoy this tale of modern architecture told through our lens.

Now we face a different future as the climate change explosion puts our island home at great risk. Understanding the enormous impact of the built environment on community, our profession must take responsibility to meet the demands of future regeneration. We hope that this book will help highlight the importance of being on the right side of this historic challenge.

As this book illustrates, AHL has met the demands of the ages with progressive ideas and innovation. We do so now recognizing the need for strong leadership and risk-taking to ensure the next 75 years will produce a built environment that addresses the economic, societal, and environmental issues we struggle with today.

We follow in the footsteps of confident and visionary leaders who shaped much of Honolulu's and Hawai'i's landscape. We hope that you, our readers, will lend us your wisdom and expertise as we face the extraordinary challenges of the next 75-year journey.

TABLE OF CONTENTS

A painting of AHL's first office – Cy Lemmon's garage on Saratoga Road.

WHERE IT ALL STARTED

When Cyril 'Cy' Lemmon opened his architectural office in 1946, his was one of around 40 such practices in the Islands. 75 years later, of those offices only his continues as an integral part of Hawai'i's architectural scene. To stay in business for such an extended period of time, the practice he started so many years ago has undergone many changes, but so too has Hawai'i. The passage of time has influenced the firm and in turn the firm has given shape to the times.

In May 1946, the 45-year-old Cy Lemmon and his wife, Rebecca, or Robbie, came to Hawai'i and in June purchased a house at 225 Saratoga Road in Waikīkī, where Trump Tower now stands. Here he set up his drafting table in the garage behind their home and opened for business. For the previous ten years Lemmon had served as a Lt. Colonel in the British Army in India, but he was not a stranger to Hawai'i. Between 1928 and 1931, he had worked as a draftsman in the Honolulu offices of both C. W. Dickey and Louis Davis, contributing to such projects as the art-deco Home Insurance Company Building and the Mediterranean-revival residence of Dr. Wall in Waimanalo.

Lemmon's timing to relocate to the Islands was ideal. Not only was there a pent-up, wartime-engendered demand for new buildings, but also Honolulu's already-growing population was set to experience even greater expansion. From the time Lemmon left Hawai'i until 1950 the population of Honolulu had increased by 74 percent, and between 1950 and 1969, when he retired, it jumped by another 79 percent.

The ambitious opportunities abounded, despite a shortage of construction materials and draftsmen. As projects came into his office, Lemmon was fortunate to convince Doug Freeth, with whom he had earlier worked in Dickey's office, to leave his job with the Federal Housing Administration, to work with him, preparing construction drawings and writing specifications. In 1948, Frank Haines, a recent graduate of M.I.T. and Princeton, was recruited, via a cousin who lived on O'ahu, to come from the mainland to further augment the staff. Both Freeth and Haines would be partners by 1953.

By that time the firm had established a solid reputation for designing in a modern style,"[1] that 'new' look which is becoming apparent to so many of Honolulu's new and remodeled shops and stores." The best of Lemmon's early buildings featured sleek horizontal lines, sometimes broken by vertical accents, built of rough textured stone contrasting with smooth concrete and large expanses of glass. He popularized the use of Arizona sandstone, a "novel treatment" that was "colorful and architecturally workable,"[2] in such early projects as the Boysen Paint Store, Konrock Building, and Occidental Life Insurance Building, making the thin-lined, horizontal material synonymous with up-to-date modern design, reaffirming the Islands' eligibility in its quest for statehood.

Another decidedly modern building, the Waikīkī-Kapahulu Library, was not only the firm's first major public works project, but also brought Wai'anae sandstone back into the public eye as a modern building material. Following its appearance in the library, this local material joined lava rock as a means to instill

Frank Haines, Paul Jones, George Woo, Joe Farrell, Rich Lowe, Doug Freeth, Alex Weinstein, Cy Lemmon, Fred White

a regional flair into Hawai'i's mid-century buildings, including the Kaimuki branch of Bishop Bank (now First Hawaiian Bank), which the firm also designed.

Lemmon, Freeth & Haines used the material again to accent the entry of the predominantly glass and brick Sinclair Library at the University of Hawai'i. Conceived as the "heart of the University"[3] and "a major step toward creating the new campus,"[4] the $1.4 million library was the largest individual building project to be initiated by the Territory in 1954, and was rushed forward in a time experiencing six percent unemployment.[5] Built with an eye to the future, the library anticipated the University's 1957 enrollment of 5,728 to more than double to 13,000 in the next ten years, which it easily surpassed, reaching 16,564 by 1967 and 21,090 by 1970, with a B. A. in pre-architecture being established in 1965, and the Department of Architecture in 1969.

An ever-expanding workload demanded additional staffing and especially a project architect, so in 1956, Paul Jones, a graduate of the University of Washington who had worked with Wimberly & Cook since his arrival to Hawai'i in 1950, was brought on board as a partner. However, instead of reducing the workload, his presence increased it as he attracted many church commissions in a time when church attendance throughout the United States was steadily growing (a 1958 Gallup poll revealed 49 percent of the nation's adult population attended church, a new high for the century6), and the newly emerging suburban communities surrounding Honolulu looked to build their own houses of worship. Jones cornered

EARLY ON THE PARTNERS AGREED TO HANDLE A DIVERSITY OF PROJECTS, RATHER THAN SPECIALIZE IN ONE AREA OF DESIGN.

the market on designing reasonably priced sanctuaries for the Lutheran, Methodist, and Presbyterian denominations, and by 1965 had designed over 30 churches, as well as the Wesley Foundation Student Center and Pohai Nani retirement home, both sponsored by the Methodist Church. His distinctive church designs skillfully ranged from the highly modern and incredibly open Kilohana United Methodist Church, to the First Presbyterian Church of Honolulu with its interpretation of traditional forms in a modern manner, to a more local variation offered by Waiokeola Congregational Church.

The office welcomed the new ecclesiastical commissions as early on the partners agreed to handle a diversity of projects, rather than specialize in one area of design, a position they have maintained until today, being equally comfortable and adept in commercial, hospitality, institutional, healthcare, education, government, and multi-family residential realms. In addition to early commercial, government, and religious commissions, the firm also received a number of jobs from developers who strove to address Honolulu's post-war housing shortage. Several of Lemmon's first commissions were for masonry, walkup apartments along the Ala Wai Canal, including the Commodore and Delgado, both of which still stand, the former on Kahakai Drive and the latter at the corner of Kaiolu and Ala Wai Boulevard. In the late 1950s and early 1960s the firm also worked on a number of garden apartments,"[6] designed for gracious living," on Pualei Circle, the only low-rise apartments in Hawai'i to receive a local AIA design award. These apartments appeared just as Honolulu's population was shifting from one of house owners to apartment dwellers, as in 1959 for the first time the number of building permits issued for apartment units exceeded those issued for single-family dwellings. This became the norm starting in 1965. In part this shift was the result of the Hawai'i Legislature's passage of laws authorizing cooperative apartment buildings in 1953, and then condominiums in 1961, which facilitated financing and made the individual possession of apartment units possible.

With an expanding demand for housing and escalating land values, high-rise living elevated the skyline of Honolulu, and Lemmon, Freeth, Haines & Jones adroitly moved from low-rise to high-rise apartments, with the 15-story Atkinson Towers Cooperative Apartments on the Ala Wai Canal being their initial foray into the realm of tall buildings. Built for Edwin Yee, it was the first in a series of projects the firm designed for the soon-to-be founder of Condominium Hawai'i, the most prolific developer of apartment buildings in Hawai'i during the 1960s. A number of these, such as the Consulate Apartments and Hale-O-Kalani Apartments broke away from the more common rectangular footprint of so many of the condominiums of the period, and their Holiday Manor was the first multi-story condominium in Hawai'i devoted exclusively to studio apartments. Its success was followed by the circular-shaped, 21-story Holiday Village, another all-studio building, which sold out in five days. With the completion of Holiday Village, Condominium Hawai'i and Lemmon, Freeth, Haines & Jones had added over 1,250 units to Honolulu's housing inventory over the course of the four-year period 1963-1967, and the architectural firm had established a reputation for handling high-rise projects.

In addition to these high-rise condominiums, the firm also designed several high-rise office buildings, including the 18-story First National (now First Hawaiian) Bank. Besides being the tallest building in downtown Honolulu upon its completion in 1962, it was also viewed as a major harbinger of the rejuvenation of downtown following retail business's shift to Ala Moana Center.

One of the first high-rise buildings in the world to use pre-stressed concrete structural members, the bank was one of a number of large projects on which Lemmon, Freeth, Haines & Jones worked under the aegis of Belt, Lemmon & Lo. To further improve the company's capabilities, in early 1955, Lemmon, Freeth & Haines entered into a joint venture with the planning firm Belt Collins and three engineering companies to form Belt, Lemmon & Lo in order to compete with mainland companies for large federal commissions. This strategy proved successful and while each firm handled their own small- to medium-sized jobs, they collaborated on a number

BELT, LEMMON & LO COULD POINT TO THEIR SUCCESSFUL FIVE YEARS OF COLLABORATION, A FACTOR THAT DID NOT GO UNNOTICED BY THE ARCHITECT SELECTION COMMITTEE.

of large-scale government projects, with Lemmon, Freeth, Haines & Jones fulfilling the architectural needs. Projects included the Capehart military housing projects at McGrew Point, Camp Catlin, Fort Shafter, and Schofield Barracks, as well as the Navy housing at Pearl City Peninsula, a hospital at Clark Air Force Base in the Philippines and an airfield at Tafuna in American Samoa. As a result of the airfield project, Lemmon, Freeth, Haines & Jones obtained a commission in 1961 to design a prototype school building for American Samoa, which was then constructed throughout the territory.

Because of Belt, Lemmon & Lo's combined staffing size and expertise they also were awarded contracts from the Territorial Department of Public Instruction to design some of their larger complexes, including Wai'anae High School, Kalani High School, and Wai'anae Intermediate School. In addition, they received the commission for Punchbowl Homes, the Hawai'i Housing Authority's first effort to provide elderly housing, and also Castle Memorial Hospital to service Windward O'ahu's growing population. By the time Lemmon stepped down as president of the consortium in 1972, they had designed over $100 million in projects.

The experience of working together during the late 1950s yielded great dividends in 1961, when Belt, Lemmon & Lo, in partnership with John Carl Warnecke, were awarded the design contract for Hawai'i's new State Capitol. While other Hawai'i architects were banding together to garner sufficient personnel to handle such a large job, Belt, Lemmon & Lo could point to their successful five years of collaboration, a factor that did not go unnoticed by the architect selection committee. With its palm tree columns rising from a reflecting pool and its central courtyard open to the sky, the elegant Capitol remains an enduring paean to Hawai'i's climate, geography, and open, hospitable style of life.

In 1961, in addition to obtaining the State Capitol commission, the joint venture also procured a second major public building contract for the design and planning of Honolulu's new federal building. However, as a result of multiple delays this project did not break ground until the end of 1972. Built around a cascading, central courtyard the building rose from four to nine stories in height accentuated by imposing cylindrical shafts. Covering an eight-acre site, the "brawny, muscular"[7] building was designed by Joe Farrell, who had joined Lemmon, Freeth, Haines & Jones in 1961, and became a partner in 1969. Employing the brutalist style of Farrell's mentor, Paul Rudolph, the giant of a building was one in a series of Farrell-engendered examples of tropical brutalism utilizing broken rib finishes. Such buildings as the Pacific Trade Center (1972), the First Federal Savings & Loan on Beretania Street (1967), the Poinciana (now Sand Villa) Hotel (1970), and the Ke'elikolani State Office Building (1986) provided Hawai'i's regional design with a new look. Upon its completion, the 30-story Pacific Trade Center was the tallest building in Hawai'i, presiding over a downtown financial district of high rises, proclaiming Honolulu's post-statehood economic progress. In addition, the Star Bulletin praised the building's "island theme,"[8] with its trellises, courtyards, and exposed Waimanalo coral limestone concrete walls, replete with petroglyphs.

Several other commissions awarded to the firm also set forth an "architecture befitting Hawai'i."[9] The Shriners Hospital (1967) with its reception area courtyard and Kapoho lava rock walls belied the anxiety of its function, while the openness of the Oahu Country Club (1970), Volcano Golf Clubhouse (1970), and First Hawaiian Bank Recreation Center (1971), all sheltered by broad, prominent roofs, led within a short few years to the design of First Hawaiian Bank's Hale'iwa branch (1976), which in 1985 received the Hawaiian Architectural Arts Award for its response to "Hawai'i's environment, culture and people."[10] The firm also displayed their cultural sensitivity, so well embedded by living in Hawai'i, further out in the Pacific, being responsible for the planning and design of the new capitol building for the Federated States of Micronesia on Pohnpei, as well as the capitol building for Palau.

Along the way, the Kona Surf Resort (1971), with its flowing indoor-outdoor relationships and murals by Tom Van Sant and Dora De Larios, further refined Hawai'i's interpretation of modern architecture in a tropical manner. The firm's first major excursion into resort design, the 550-room hotel added another dimension to the company's portfolio, while momentarily providing the island of Hawai'i with its largest hotel, a major step forward in the visitor industry's expansion to the neighbor islands.

These excursions into brutalism and a more regional approach were contemporaneous with a pair of condominium projects, the Barclay Apartments (1969) and the 569-unit Marco Polo Apartments (1971), the largest condominium of its time in Hawai'i. With their serrated and S-curve footprints, they continued the company's move away from the stereotypical high rise box. Fred White, who had designed the Kona Surf, as well as the Barclay Apartments, further extended this impetus with 1010 Wilder (1974), with its large lanai and dramatically cantilevered upper stories. "The ultimate in condominium living,"[11] the top half of the 18-story building held only two units per floor, with an elevator at either end of the building opening directly into the unit.

In addition to changes wrought by larger commissions and new design approaches, other changes were also transpiring within Lemmon, Freeth, Haines & Jones itself. Cy Lemmon stepped down as president of the firm in 1969, and Frank Haines took over the reins, inheriting a staff of 46 who generated gross billings of almost two million dollars a year. Over the course of the next few years the number of staff, associates, and partners increased to such a degree that in 1976 the largest architectural firm in the State was renamed Architects Hawaii, with Frank Haines, Paul Jones, Joe Farrell, Fred White, Stanley Gima, Alex Weinstein, and David Miller all principals in the company which now numbered over 60 employees, including 16 registered architects.

Following the name change, and the celebration of 30 years of practice, the firm continued to grow and build on its past experience by taking on larger projects in such diverse fields as healthcare, education, high-rise offices, resort hotels, and condominiums. In addition, they started to work with the emerging realm of international investors interested in undertaking development projects in Hawai'i.

Gary Marshall joined the firm in 1978 and became a senior associate in 1982. A specialist in hospital and institutional design, he expanded the firm's position in the healthcare field, which was already well established by such projects as Shriners Hospital, Castle Hospital, and a new wing and administration building for Straub Clinic. Thanks to Marshall's presence the firm provided Queens Hospital with a major updating and expansion, and also designed Kaiser's new hospital at Red Hill, as well as medical facilities for Adventist Health Services Asia in Singapore, Penang, Karachi, and Hong Kong (1992–1996) and the distinctive, multi-pastel-colored Kameda Medical Center in Japan (1989–2004). In addition, with the Kaiser Permanente Honolulu Clinic on King Street (1986), Marshall provided Honolulu with not only a striking view of architecture's emerging Late Modern sensibility but also a newly conceived energy efficiency consciousness. The design's distinctive light shelves extended from the exterior front windows to shade the lower two thirds of the window and reflect light up to the interior ceilings resulting in about a 30 percent energy savings, at least two decades before LEED became a buzzword.[12]

With Pioneer Plaza (1977) and Grosvenor Center's two mirror-clad towers (1979–1983) Architects Hawaii placed an exclamation point on a decade of office-tower development in downtown

Left to right: Charles (Chuck) Ehron, David Miller, Mel Roop

Honolulu, and marked the conclusion of the redevelopment of the city's financial core. The latter, designed by Joe Farrell, was the largest commercial office space in Hawai'i for its time,

ITS UNDULATING FAÇADE AND EYE-CATCHING THREE-STORY WATERFALL DISPLAY WINDOWS NOT ONLY HELPED INTRODUCE LATE MODERN ARCHITECTURE TO HONOLULU, BUT ALSO COMMENCED ARCHITECTS HAWAII'S LONG-RUNNING RELATIONSHIP WITH JAPANESE INVESTORS INTERESTED IN DEVELOPING PROJECTS IN HAWAI'I.

while the former marked a new direction for Architects Hawaii: working in collaboration with outside architects, in this instance Gerald Kremkow of Pioneer Properties Inc, to help develop well-conceived buildings.

A third commercial project of the period was the nine-story Rainbow Promenade (1979) in Waikīkī, designed by Fred White. The building, with its undulating façade and eye-catching three-story waterfall display windows, not only helped introduce Late Modern architecture to Honolulu, but also commenced Architects Hawaii's long-running relationship with Japanese investors interested in developing projects in Hawai'i.

The firm also continued to build on its reputation for quality condominium designs, becoming a major player in the realm of luxury living with the low-rise Ironwoods at Kapalua, Maui (1979), designed by David Miller working with Eric Engstrom and Ted Garduque; and Kuumakana (1981), on Diamond Head, designed by Frank Haines; as well as the high-rise Liliuokalani Gardens (1984), designed by Fred White. The former involved the development of 40 high-end units in ten, two- to three-story beach front buildings, and was described by the Los Angeles Times as "designed to bring real luxury back to the leisure class"[13] Thirty-one of the units were sold over the course of a cocktail party, for the then unimaginably high price of approximately $442,000 per unit, at a time when a similar unit in the leasehold Kahala Beach Apartments was selling for around $220,000. Within a year, the selling price of the latter had risen to match or surpass that of Ironwoods. Miller, a graduate of Carnegie Mellon and Harvard, worked for SOM prior to joining Lemmon, Freeth, Haines & Jones in 1971.

Liliuokalani Gardens' twin towers occupied a 2.5-acre block with 70 percent in a "park-like" open space. The 382-unit complex was only the second condominium project approved in Waikīkī during the eight years following the passage of the 1976 Waikīkī Special Design District ordinance, with its goal to soften Waikīkī's "concrete jungle" image. Like the Rainbow Promenade, the project was undertaken by a Japanese development company. Following Japan's joining the Organization of Economic Cooperation and Development in 1964, Japan loosened first its foreign travel and then capital movement policies, which by 1975 resulted in Japanese visitors comprising 22 percent of Hawai'i's tourism mix. Investment followed with a spurt of investment in the early 1970s and then a second wave at the end of the decade, in which the Rainbow Promenade and Queen Liliuokalani Gardens figured prominently.

Another Japanese-backed project undertaken by White was the 19-story Tokai University (1990). With its pure-white masonry walls and blocky massing softened by rounded corners, trellises, and recessed banks of windows, the building followed the stylistic manner of a number of buildings and hospitals on the University's Japan campuses, presenting Honolulu with yet another version of Late Modern slick tech design. The fascination with slick tech continued with Alex Weinstein's Waikīkī Landmark (1993), which was also developed with Japanese investment funds. With its red-tinted granite and aquamarine and mauve glass twin towers connected by a dramatic six-story bridge, starting at the 33rd floor, this mixed-use condominium included 196 luxury apartments set on a lot with 64 percent of the land dedicated to open space. Pulling building permits in March 1991, the Waikīkī Landmark was part of the greatest building boom in Hawai'i's history to that point, with building permits for that month topping $400 million, an all-time monthly high, which more than doubled the island's previous monthly totals.

The late-20th-century projects opened the doors for Architects Hawaii's large presence in the high-rise luxury condominium market which exploded during the opening decades of the 21st century, starting with Laniakea (2005), one of the first condominium projects to be built in Waikīkī, since the opening of the Waikīkī Landmark more than a decade earlier. Others followed, capitalizing on a real estate market, which saw approximately 28 percent of all residential purchases in Hawai'i made by high-end mainland or foreign investors during the years 2008–2015. The glass-sheathed, elliptical cylinders of Moana Pacifica (2007) with their million-dollar units continued the trend of high-end condominiums catering to off-shore investors seeking a piece of Hawai'i's ever-upward-spiraling real estate market. In the following year the Watermark (2008) introduced "an urban eclecticism tempered with the warmth of Hawai'i's best traditional architecture, breaking new design ground while retaining a measure of island-style comfort and familiarity,"[14] Other exercises in luxury living followed: Allure Waikīkī (2009); and then Pacifica (2012) with its "cross braced" homage to I. M. Pei's Bank of China in Hong Kong; and then Symphony (2016), designed in collaboration with Gensler, with David Miller and Daniel Moats leading the project for Architects Hawaii. The latter's lanai-studded, sky-blending tower rose from a podium housing Velocity's auto showroom. This project was followed by Ae'o (2019) with Whole Foods as a podium anchor, and designed in collaboration with the mainland firm of Bohlin Cywinsky Jackson, further adding to the ever-growing skyline of Kaka'ako.

Keeping with the belief that the needs of the client and project should generate an appropriate design, Architects Hawaii did not adhere to any specific style of building, and thus were among the first in Honolulu to sojourn into the realm of Post Modern design. In some instances their designs were pushed by historic preservation concerns for compatibility with existing building stock as in the case of the Harold K. L. Castle Memorial Building at the Bishop Museum (1983), or by City and County design guidelines as in Marin Tower (1994) and the "friendly-looking" Kapolei police station (2000) designed by Tom Young. However, the firm's Waialae Building (1990) in Kaimuki, designed by Alex Weinstein, with its segmental arches, recessed loggias, and double-hung sash windows, broke new ground, being among the first Post Modern buildings in Hawai'i to be developed outside the purview of government design directions.

In response to changing cultural landscape and the fading influence of Post Modernism, AHL began to design in a more sensitive, and regionally influenced form of modernism. This transformation is announced in the beginning of the 21st century in such resort retail projects as the Shops at Wailea (2000), Shops at Mauna Lani (2006), and the Shops at Kukui'ula (2009). Handled by David Miller, who had become CEO of Architects Hawaii in 2000, these complexes provided the consumption-conscious visitor trade with a charming, upscale environment, and set a tone for others to follow. The Shops at Mauna Lani joined Lanikea, to signal a re-emerging confidence in Hawai'i's tenuous post–Twin Towers economy.

This new Regional Modernism also injected new life into the institutional and government commissions that also appeared, including: the Kāhala Nui senior living development (2005), the Burns School of Medicine (2005) designed by Walter Muraoka, the Center of Waikīkī (2007), Ronald T.Y. Moon Judiciary Complex (2010) designed by David Bylund, and the library at Windward Community College (2012) designed by Stan Yasumoto. The Family Court and the FBI Field Office (2012), along with the earlier police station, helped foster Kapolei's image as O'ahu's "second city," which would be solidified by the Ka Makana Ali'i shopping center with its 150 shops and restaurants (2018), which design architect Emile Alano and Lester Ng rendered in a more contemporary regional vocabulary.

In addition to making major contributions to Kapolei, the firm helped place Ko Olina on the map as a resort destination with the development of the resort destination's second and third major hotels: Marriott's Ko Olina Beach Club (2003) with its four V-shaped towers housing 750 two- and three-bedroom time-share units, and Disney's Hawaiian-themed Aulani (2011), on which the firm collaborated with Disney's Imagineering Team and WATG. The presence of these visitor accommodations solidified Ko Olina as a viable destination resort, further contributing to the development of the west end of the O'ahu.

With Hawai'i's population jumping by nearly one million since the 1950 census count of 498,000, the Islands have gone through many profound changes. Gone is the gentler

Waikīkī of Cy Lemmon working on architectural commissions out of his garage. Indeed, the sight of a detached garage has completely vanished from Waikīkī's landscape, and in its stead has emerged a world-class urban resort replete with a high-rise skyline, to which AHL has significantly contributed over the years.

As Hawai'i has grown and expanded its role in the world, so too AHL has continually evolved to meet the needs of Hawai'i. Thanks to its wide range of projects and diverse client base, AHL has impacted almost every aspect of Hawai'i's built environment, from Keauhou to Ko Olina. Working with people from around the globe to design a gamut of buildings from schools and government buildings, to religious and medical facilities, to high-rise offices and condominiums, to single family dwellings, the firm has leant an important hand in shaping the physical world in which the people of Hawai'i today live. It has grown from a small office designing low-rise buildings that celebrated a modern tropical paradise worthy of statehood, to become a multi-faceted organization capable of overseeing the design and construction of complex, large-scale projects, increasingly in collaboration with other architects and designers. These projects serve not only the people of Hawai'i, but also address the international market of which the Islands are now a part. The firm serves as a bridge, meeting the needs of the modern world while remaining ever mindful of the special place we call home, with its distinct culture, traditions, and ways of life. •

REFERENCES

1 - [Honolulu Advertiser, March 21, 1948]

2 - [Star Bulletin, October 2, 1948, p.6]

3 - [Advertiser, July 7, 1954, p. 13]

4 - [Star Bulletin, May 28, 1953]

5 - [Advertiser, May 8, 1954, p. 9]

6 - [Star Bulletin, January 3, 1959, p. 13]

7 - [Advertiser, July 26, 1974, p. B1]

8 - [Star Bulletin, June 6, 1971, p. B8]

9 - [Honolulu Star Advertiser, March 12, 1967, p. 8]

10 - [Advertiser, December 1, 1986]

11 - [Star Bulletin, July 9, 1972]

12 - [Star Bulletin, July 25, 1986, p. A10]

13 - [Los Angeles Times, October 22, 1978, p. 104]

14 - [Advertiser, November 6, 2005, p.R21]

1946–1950

BORN IN A GARAGE

Hawai'i was recovering. It was 1946. Hawai'i and the world were recovering from World War II and with regular airline service restored, Waikīkī was once again seeing an influx of visitors with many choosing to stay permanently. The war had introduced Hawai'i to countless servicemen and women, and many chose to call the islands their home now that Hawai'i was headed toward statehood.

Born in England, Cy Lemmon was educated and worked on the US mainland. As a young architect Cy's travels led him to Hawai'i before World War II where he worked on some of Hawai'i's notable public buildings including Honolulu's City Hall. After serving in the British military in India during the Second World War, Cy returned to Honolulu and opened his practice in his garage on Saratoga Road, Waikīkī. Starting with residences, he was soon selected to create a master plan for a resort complex at Coconut Island in Kāne'ohe Bay, and began recruiting key staff with the addition of Doug Freeth and Frank Haines.

Cy's vision was to build a firm to serve the territory of Hawai'i that in the foreseeable future would become the 50th state. Cy understood that a new state would need many types of new buildings from residential and commercial to medical care, educational, hospitality, plus State City and Federal projects of all size. With this strategy he began to grow an architectural firm that could flourish with the state and provide design services to meet Hawai'i's diverse future needs.

BOYSEN PAINT COMPANY

COMPLETED **1949**

Construction of Kapi'olani Boulevard began in 1931 to connect downtown Honolulu to Waikīkī, but it wasn't until the conclusion of WWII that the humble stretch of road genuinely developed as a commercial corridor.

Retail stores began lining either side, with individual store parking lots on the front, side, or rear, catering more to automobile customers rather than pedestrian traffic. The thoroughfare quickly became labeled "The Miracle Mile" because of its similarities to the highly successful two-mile stretch of Wilshire Boulevard in Los Angeles. Stores typically were designed with extended buildings oriented towards the street to appeal to the vehicular traffic, with simple signage and ornamentation easily recognized by those passing by at a higher rate of speed.

These low-rise buildings were a change from the typical vertical orientation of the downtown retail stores.

In 1949, the firm built its first significant commercial building along this newly thriving commercial corridor. Designed by Cy Lemmon, the building's tall vertical feature wall created a striking element that became a significant landmark for customers driving by along Kapi'olani Boulevard. Lemmon appreciated the roughness of the surface of Arizona sandstone and the effect created with the horizontal cut of the stone and used it on the finish of the building. The exterior embodies strong vertical and horizontal contrasts, comprising the flat horizontal roof supported by heavy vertical elements, and the prominent vertical feature wall dividing the building. The full-height windows along the street side and

BOYSEN
PAINTS

parking area allow an unobstructed view into the building interior. The sandstone-clad feature wall displayed neon signage reading "Boysen Paints," in clear view for all potential passing customers. The interior display area contained a slate floor and a ceiling element with lights arranged in the shape of a paint palette. •

PROJECT CREDITS

ARCHITECT
Cyril W. Lemmon

STATE OF HAWAI'I PUBLIC SCHOOLS

COMPLETED **1958–1962**

King Kamehameha III established free public schools in Hawai'i in 1840. It is the only educational system in the United States founded by a sovereign monarch and the oldest educational system west of the Mississippi.

Teachers initially taught their students in Hawaiian, but as foreign influence in economics and politics increased, English became the primary language of instruction.

In the late 1960s and early 70s, there was concern that the culture of the Hawaiian people was at risk of disappearing. This fear sparked a major movement of local support for Hawaiian music, hula, and language. In 1978 the State constitution was amended to officially recognize Hawaiian as one of the two official state languages in Hawai'i.

Leading up to this movement was Honolulu's accelerating growth during the 1950s and 60s. This growth created an equally urgent demand for new public schools. The City & County appointed Lemmon, Freeth & Haines, and its affiliate Belt, Lemmon & Lo to develop a comprehensive master plan for the future of education in the new state. The plan included elementary, intermediate, and high schools; athletic fields; parks and recreation areas; and future faculty housing. The City & County selected Belt, Lemmon & Lo as architects engineers for four new major public schools. Wai'anae High School, Wai'anae Intermediate School, Kalani High School, and James Campbell High School.

The Wai'anae campus design included multiple low-rise concrete buildings with elongated, rectangular massing. Wai'anae's frequently dry, hot climate required the orientation of all buildings to take full advantage of the northeast trade winds. The design of the wide overhanging eaves and continuous bands of louvered windows keep the buildings cool. Despite restrictive design

guidelines, the firm achieved an aesthetically pleasing building that incorporated residential elements, like wood louvers, into the concrete structure as well as the first internal drainage system to be used in an education building in Hawai'i. Kalani High and James Campbell High used a similar overall design approach.

Kalani High School opened in 1958. Facilities comprised nine main buildings, a physical education facility, cafeteria, gymnasium, several portable buildings, a large building for their musical department, a swimming pool, sports courts, and athletic field.

James Campbell High School in Ewa Beach opened in 1962, serving seven rural and two military communities. The school included 11 predominant main buildings and an athletic complex on 38 acres. It offers a combination of comprehensive vocational, technical, academic, and special education programs.

Together, these four campuses, still in use today, form the mid-century modern core of Hawai'i's public education system expansion. Many of the sustainable design principles utilized to inform the building design, orientation, and massing are equally relevant now as they were then.•

PROJECT CREDITS

CLIENT
City & County of Honolulu

ARCHITECT
Lemmon, Freeth & Haines
Belt, Lemmon & Lo

1950–1962

A NEW STATE

Hawai'i was changing. Businesses were expanding along with a growing population that needed more services, more homes, more infrastructure, more everything. AHL satisfied this diverse need by designing places of worship, places to live, places for business, learning, and healing.

As envisioned, the firm's diverse marketing strategy began to bear fruit in 1948 when the firm was selected to design a new office development on Honolulu's Kapi'olani Boulevard. Named the Kenrock Building, the office was designed to be built in phases and Cy quickly moved the office into the ground floor of the first phase in 1948. Kapi'olani's commercial growth accelerated quickly due to its central location between downtown and Waikīkī. By the time the Kenrock Building was fully complete, the firm had grown substantially and moved to a large space on the second floor where the firm remained till 1962. The firm, then named Lemmon, Freeth, Haines & Jones, was now well positioned and contributing to the rapid growth of Honolulu.

With no architecture school in the state, trained draftsmen and other project staff were scarce and the firm embraced an entrepreneurial attitude finding talented individuals from diverse backgrounds. Together, the trained architects learned how to become teachers who could guide and encourage the staff that grew with them. During those years, several of the firm's significant projects included University of Hawai'i's Sinclair Library, Occidental Life Insurance Headquarters, Wai'anae High School, Borthwick Mortuary, and numerous churches throughout O'ahu.

1394
OUT

KENROCK BUILDING

COMPLETED

1948

BRAINARD & BLACK
Insurance Exclusively
KENROCK BUILDING
HONOLULU ROOFING Co., LTD.

DESIGNED JUST THREE YEARS AFTER AHL'S FOUNDING IN 1946, KENROCK BUILDING'S THREE TWO-STORY STRUCTURES' OVERALL PLAN WAS CONSTRUCTED IN PHASES, RESPONDING TO HONOLULU'S EVOLVING COMMERCIAL GROWTH.

1392
KENROCK
BUILDING
HONOLULU ROOFING CO., LTD.

From the late 1940s, Honolulu's Kapi'olani Boulevard was anticipated as a main thoroughfare, linking Downtown and Government Center with Waikīkī, and considered Honolulu's "Miracle Mile of the 1950s."

PROJECT CREDITS

ARCHITECT
Cyril W. Lemmon & Douglas Freeth

CONTRACTOR
Pacific Construction Co.

The Kenrock Building's three two-story structures' overall plan was constructed in phases, responding to Honolulu's evolving commercial growth and was designed just three years after the firm's founding in 1946. Kenrock's initial phase in 1950 was a portion of the first structure, fully completed in 1951. That year, the firm moved from its founder Cy Lemmon's garage in Waikīkī's Lewers Street into a 900-square-foot Kenrock ground-floor space as an initial tenant.

The entire three-building Kenrock complex was completed in 1958, timed with completion of the soon-to-be nationally prominent shopping center nearby at Kapi'olani Boulevard's considerable crossroads. From its opening in 1959, Ala Moana Shopping Center became the largest shopping mall in the US, sparking a significant increase in Honolulu's vehicular shopping pattern. By the time of Ala Moana Shopping Center's opening, the firm had grown significantly and taken a sizable upper floor space in Kenrock.

With its elongated low profile, ashlar masonry base, and thin concrete slab projections, Kenrock's imagery conveys understated elegance and stylistic fashion for a timeless aesthetic. At the onset of its initial phase in 1950, Kenrock Building's mid-century design received recognition and compliments. In that year, Architectural Forum, the country's premier design publication, praised the Kenrock Building as one of Hawai'i's most beautiful buildings.

Cy Lemmon's visionary move into Kenrock reinforced the firm's brand both regarding modernist design and highly efficient and functional retail and commercial projects. AHL's move into Kenrock marked a tradition of AHL firm's offices in its endeavors, a tradition now for over 75 years with six locational office moves and its current 31st Floor location at the top of 733 Bishop Street's Pacific Guardian Tower.

Demolished in 2020 to make room for a nondescript residential tower, "The Kenrock" as it is affectionately known within the office, will always have a special place within the firm's and the design community's collective memory. Its loss shall also serve as a reminder to the community about the importance of incorporating the past with the future in all projects. •

ATKINSON TOWERS

COMPLETED **1959**

PROJECT CREDITS

CLIENT
Edwin K. Q. Yee, Atkinson Towers

ARCHITECT
Lemmon, Freeth, Haines & Jones

CONTRACTOR
Pacific Construction Company

September 6, 1959, marked a significant day for Honolulu's emerging urban development. Joined by George Freitas of Pacific Construction Co. and Edwin Yee of Atkinson Towers, Inc., architect Frank Haines participated in the monumental groundbreaking for Atkinson Towers along the banks of the Ala Wai Canal.

The building marked a compelling shift in urban development and, upon completion, was Waikīkī's tallest building at 14 stories. With full construction costs estimated at $2,769,800, the Atkinson Towers became the first residential co-operative in Honolulu.

Designed by Lemmon, Freeth, Haines & Jones, Atkinson Towers became the model for a multitude of high-rise residential developments that followed in the 1950s and beyond. Its 104 two-bedroom apartments each had its parking stall. Kitchens situated adjacent to the lanai incorporated aluminum sliding screens to address glaring afternoon sun. Each unit came equipped with a pastel-colored General Electric kitchen center that included an automatic dishwasher, garbage disposal, and stainless-steel sinks. The sliding fusuma doors at each side of the family room allowed for modular conversion to a guest room when needed. Sliding doors between the lanai and living room allowed for complete flexibility that could open the entire unit. Units also boasted air conditioners. In addition to an "exotic free-form" swimming pool with changing facilities, a boat landing was also incorporated on the Ala Wai Canal, for residents' "sailing, fishing, or water-skiing pleasure."

The building's residents had control over the management of the property through full and equal voting rights and were stockholders in the co-operative corporation. At the time Atkinson Towers was constructed, co-operative apartments dramatically changed the lives and living habits of people on O'ahu, perhaps more than any other single building development. In a 1959 newspaper article, retired couples describe the time saved with freedom from yard work and house maintenance. Young professionals and newlyweds focused on their active lives, and were relieved from paying utility, garbage, and other bills.

Atkinson Towers' developer, Edwin Yee, was destined to become Hawai'i's dominant middle-income residential developer, teaming with Lemmon, Freeth, Haines & Jones on a multitude of multifamily projects throughout Honolulu through the 1960s and 1970s. •

MOKU O LOʻE

"COCONUT ISLAND"

COMPLETED **1950**

Moku o lo'e (Coconut Island) is situated on O'ahu's Windward side sheltered by Kane'ohe Bay with panoramic views of O'ahu's mountains and beachfront. Moku o lo'e, initially owned by the Bishop Estate, is called Coconut Island as it is lined with coconut trees.

Princess Bernice Pauahi Bishop planted the trees to honor Queen Emma's lifetime achievements. Local fishermen used the island as a base.

The Coconut Island Club International has significant meaning for AHL as it was a notable major early commission for Cy Lemmon's young design firm.

Coconut Island's unique history picks up in 1934 when the picturesque island was acquired by Chris Holmes II, heir to the Fleishmann's Yeast fortune. Using coral rubble, sand, and earthen landfill, Holmes doubled the island's size from 12 to 24 acres, creating extensive palm-fringed lagoons. He built a mansion with kennels, aviaries, and fishponds that would later be of great use to the Hawai'i Marine Lab. Holmes kept several exotic animals, and after his death, these animals became the beginnings of the Honolulu Zoo.

After the Pearl Harbor attack in 1941, Holmes turned the island over to the military for an R&R station for officers. They built barracks that eventually became the Hawai'i Marine Lab. Chris Holmes passed away at a young age during the war, and in 1946 a group of five Los Angeles businessmen, headed by wealthy oilman Edwin Pauley, bought the island from his estate. Investors envisioned the development of a private, members-only community of cottages, tennis courts, a yacht club, and recreational facilities, including

remodeling the Holmes mansion and barracks. Eventually, Pauley bought out the interest of the other four, becoming sole owner of the island.

In 1947, Cy Lemmon's architectural firm was commissioned together with architects Paul Williams and A. Quincy Jones. Brought in by the client, these Los Angeles-based architects had established reputations, including designing homes for Hollywood celebrities.

Various uses and activities took place on the island over time. In 1948 the Pauley family donated a portion of the island to the University of Hawai'i for a marine research facility.

Following design and planning, the original vision for the community was reduced and redefined in 1949. The Coconut Island Club and Hotel opened in February 1950, offering a luxury "tropical retreat" experience for 32 guests.

In 1961, the original Hawai'i Marine Lab building burned down. Pauley donated funds toward reconstruction of the present structure, completed in 1965, and formally renamed it Hawai'i Institute of Marine Biology (HIMB).

In 1964, the highly popular "Gilligan's Island" TV sitcom premiered, using Coconut Island for its opening sequence. Subsequently, the hotel became known as "Coconut Gilligan's Island Club Hawai'i." From then to the mid-1980s, the Pauley family used the island for summer getaways.

After Edwin Pauley died in 1981, the property was on the market. Katsuhiro Kawaguchi paid $8.5 million in cash for a portion of the island, with the understanding that he would continue to provide support and funding to HIMB. In 1995, the Pauley family donated funds to the UH Foundation to purchase the portion of the island owned by Kawaguchi. The island is now entirely owned by the State of Hawai'i and houses the HIMB, the only US laboratory built on a coral reef.

As with many commissions, AHL's work on Coconut Island began with a client's big vision. Also, as with many commissions, the overall project never came fully into reality. But although the architects' work over roughly two years resulted in a smaller project, Coconut Island Club International's presence in Hawai'i and beyond was a significant step forward in reinforcing Cy Lemmon's young architectural practice's presence throughout Hawai'i's community overall. •

PROJECT CREDITS

CLIENT

The Queen's Health Systems

ARCHITECT

Cyril W. Lemmon, Paul Williams, and A. Quincy Jones

CAPEHART HOUSING

COMPLETED **1955–1964**

PROJECT CREDITS

ARCHITECT
Lemmon, Freeth & Haines;
Lemmon, Freeth, Haines & Jones

Following World War II, approximately 15 million service members returned to the US to restart their lives in society. Even though the country was officially at peace, the looming political issues of the Cold War required that a large number of military personnel be available.

Affordable housing shortages were widespread, as military bases all over the country were not prepared to handle the surge in population.

The government instituted two programs to address the housing shortage; the first was created by Senator Kenneth Wherry of Nebraska, who introduced a bill in 1949 to build military housing on bases throughout the US. From this program, 264 Wherry projects were constructed, totaling over 83,000 units. More accommodation was still required, so Senator Homer Capehart from Indiana led a second effort. The Capehart housing act was passed in 1955 and allowed for more spacious floor plans combined with newer building restrictions. Privacy, preservation of the natural environment, and integration of the neighborhood into existing facilities were crucial issues, as well as a move towards more single-family and duplex housing. From 1950 through 1964, Wherry and Capehart housing produced a total of nearly 250,000 units, helping meet a critical need at a time of a severe national housing shortage.

The first Capehart housing project for the firm was in 1955 at McGrew point in Pearl Harbor. It was the first of many military housing projects that the firm designed as part of the Belt, Lemmon & Lo association.

The firm designed several Capehart housing projects in Hawai'i, including a 922-unit project comprised of single and duplex units in Pearl Harbor in 1958. Deviation from the multi-unit design increased the site development cost and land requirements, and conventional local single-board redwood construction managed to keep the overall cost within very tight limitations.

Another 1964 Capehart project entailed 500 units located at Pearl City, Kane'ohe, Camp Smith, and Pearl Harbor. The project retained and took advantage of the many mature existing trees on the site, enhancing the family living environment. •

OCCIDENTAL LIFE INSURANCE BUILDING

COMPLETED **1951 / 1967** Addition

Founded in 1933 by Lawrence Takeo Kagawa as the Security Insurance Agency, Occidental Insurance contributed significantly to Hawai'i's development and growth.

Representing Occidental Life Insurance of California, Occidental was acquired in 1930 by Bank of America's then holding company, Transamerica Corporation. It received its current name, Occidental Underwriters of Hawaii, in 1954 and has remained one of Hawai'i's largest insurance companies to the present day.

In the early 1950s, Occidental selected Lemmon, Freeth, Haines & Jones as the architect for their new two-story building at Honolulu's prominent Beretania and Pi'ikoi Streets corner. Then-president, Lawrence Kagawa, was a visionary and believed in the effects of design on communities and people. Lemmon, Freeth, Haines & Jones's "Hawai'i Modernist" design approach was carried out with collaborative interaction with Kagawa, creating unique office spaces. Kagawa envisioned more than the conventional office layout, he wanted to provide a welcoming interior environment for the customers complete with full carpet and a hospitality-inspired "living lounge." The collaboration between client, architect, and interior designer created a striking design that was recognized in Hawai'i and abroad. In 1953, the notable French design magazine "L'Architecture d'Aujourd'hui" featured the Occidental Life Building in a 26-page spread.

As Transamerica's prominence grew nationally, so did Occidental's in Hawai'i. Both Transamerica and Occidental shared the commitment to expressing their brand through their innovative building designs. Transamerica's iconic pyramid in San Francisco started construction in 1969, virtually at the same time Occidental commenced construction in Hawai'i of Lemmon, Freeth, Haines & Jones's iconic "Bird's Nest" addition.

OCCIDENTAL LIFE

The development housed Chairman Kagawa's offices. Other innovative design concepts for the project included open, casual sales staff work areas rather than private offices; tables rather than desks; and a centralized, relaxed lounge area. The completed spaces provided a collaborative work environment that encouraged teamwork and fostered improved social interactions for employees and customers.

AHL takes pride in the fact that the Occidental Life Insurance Building continues to serve its founding owners, Occidental Underwriters of Hawaii, as it has for over 60 years. •

PROJECT CREDITS

CLIENT
Occidental Life Insurance

ARCHITECT
Lemmon, Freeth, Haines & Jones

ASSOCIATE ARCHITECT
Ernest Hara

INTERIOR DESIGN
Jan Hombeck

CONTRACTOR
Thomas T. Tanaka

UNIVERSITY OF HAWAIʻI

SINCLAIR LIBRARY

COMPLETED **1956**

The Gregg M. Sinclair Library was the firm's first higher educational facility commission and the first significant building constructed at the University after World War II.

The planning process began in 1951 with architects Lemmon, Freeth & Haines to prepare the plans. Cy Lemmon served as the design architect. In 1951, Lemmon and University Librarian Dr. Carl Stroven traveled to the US mainland to research various libraries in preparation for the new Library. They spent considerable time studying libraries for both student and public use. Lemmon also worked closely with the members of the library staff, library committee, and administrative staff.

Several cost issues arose in the planning process. The 1953 Hawai'i State Legislature allocated $1.4 million to the construction budget; however, there was still a budget shortfall for the approved design. As a result, the building size was reduced by removing the top floor and shortening the two main volumes of the building. With an eye toward future expansion, the building design afforded the addition of two stories added later. Another issue affecting the plan was air conditioning. The State of Hawai'i wouldn't allow for air conditioning as they determined it would be too expensive to maintain. This factor created the difficult design challenge of constructing an immense institutional building in the tropics that was comfortable without air conditioning. Solutions included decisions based on shading, light, airflow, and orientation.

During the planning phase, the Honolulu Advertiser called the library "One of America's Finest." The groundbreaking for Sinclair Library was on July 6, 1954, with Ben Hayashi Construction Co. serving as contractor. Lemmon adhered to several basic principles in the design of the Library. He said,

> "*It must be made as comfortable for readers as possible without air conditioning and arranged for efficient operation. It must be flexible enough to be readily adapted to changing needs and conceptions of service, and to make books and other library materials as accessible and convenient for use as possible.*"

In addition to three stacks, the Library featured an audio-visual center, reading rooms, reserve rooms, administrative offices, and a Teachers College Library on the main floor. The library massing has two large rectangular elements that intersect on a perpendicular axis. Multiple smaller components overlap both horizontally and vertically at each façade. A wide overhanging canopy at the entrance provides a sculptural feature to the building in contrast to the overall cubic massing. The exterior finishes include plastered concrete, Wai'anae sandstone, and Roman brick veneer. The entrance area finish is sandstone rubble masonry. Horizontal bands of aluminum jalousies stretch along most of the façade at the second and third floors facing Campus Road to provide much-needed light and ventilation.

The Gregg M. Sinclair Library opened in 1956 and remains a popular destination for UH students, faculty, and staff. •

PROJECT CREDITS

CLIENT
University of Hawai'i

ARCHITECT
Lemmon, Freeth & Haines

CONTRACTOR
Ben Hayashi Construction Company

TOWERS AT KŪHIŌ PARK

COMPLETED

1965 NEW CONSTRUCTION / **2013** RENOVATION

In 1962 Governor John Burns announced the State's intention to build a significant affordable housing project in Honolulu.

The State selected Lemmon, Freeth, Haines & Jones, and their consortium of Belt, Lemmon & Lo as architects.

Named Kūhiō Park Terrace, construction of the 572-unit twin 16-story residential towers was completed with move-ins commencing in 1964. Kūhiō Park Terrace was part of a national publicly funded housing effort that began during the Great Depression and accelerated following WWII with the passage of the Federal Housing Act of 1949. New York City Mayor Fiorello LaGuardia was a leader, and New York City led the country in this development. Most of the postwar projects, built in the modernist, tower-in-the-park style popular at that time, had over 1,000 apartment units.

By the end of the 1960s, many of the large, modernist tower public housing projects in major cities proved problematic as tight operating budgets, impersonal living environments, and security issues took their toll, including Kūhiō Park Terrace.

Kūhiō Park Terrace's additional issue was the change of living environment Hawai'i residents experienced transitioning from rural low-rise to high-density urban high-rise living. While much of the population enthusiastically welcomed the many new market-rate high-rise living environments in Honolulu, the dramatic lifestyle change proved especially challenging for Hawai'i's lower-income families.

From its 1965 opening, Kūhiō Park Terrace continued providing affordable housing for Hawai'i's families. During the next 40 years, the State considered new ideas and approaches to improve their quality of life. In 2009 the Hawaii Public Housing Authority selected the New Jersey–based Michaels Organization together with the Vitus Group to undertake a $316 million

Photo: Bad Moon Saloon / Max Kim

redevelopment for one-for-one replacement of Kūhiō Park Terrace's affordable housing units plus the addition of 276 subsidized, senior, and market rental units.

AHL was again chosen as architects to create a project vision for "transformation into a vibrant, mixed-income, financially viable, supportive community that is the pride of residents and the Kalihi neighborhood." AHL's design approach entailed maintaining the existing tower structures, full renovation of all units, and phased construction to minimize relocation of existing tenants.

Extensive interviews and meetings with residents enabled AHL designers to understand their wishes and desires. "Wish lists" focused on providing more green open space, community gardens, expanded laundry facilities, gathering places, and a safer, cleaner overall environment. New services included a fitness center, technology Center, Literary Family Library, and the Ke Ola Hou Medical Clinic. The building's exterior aesthetics featured enhancements of decorative rails and grilles, a two-color façade scheme, and newly enclosed balconies adding interior apartment space. Sustainable strategies combined utilizing prevailing trade winds; natural light and ventilation; green building techniques and materials; photovoltaic; and low impact, indigenous landscaping.

In 2013, upon completion of the project, refreshed and rejuvenated, Kūhiō Park Terrace became known as The Towers at Kūhiō Park. Programming and overall exterior and interior changes achieved the project's goals of "transformation," and "The Towers at Kūhiō Park" has been well received by residents and the Kalihi community overall. In 2013 Michaels Development received the National Affordable Housing Management Association's Award for Revitalization. •

PROJECT CREDITS

CLIENT

State of Hawai'i Public Housing Authority and Michaels Development Company

ARCHITECT

Lemmon, Freeth, Haines & Jones; AHL

CONTRACTOR

Albert C. Kobayashi, Inc.

WAIKĪKĪ-KAPAHULU LIBRARY

COMPLETED **1952**

The Waikīkī-Kapahulu Library was the first public building project for the firm. Frank Haines noted that the library was "one of the most significant buildings the firm had designed in the early days."

Located at the edge of Waikīkī where Kapahulu Avenue meets the Ala Wai, the only library previously in the area was housed in a small cottage that provided books to school children. The library opened in July 1952 to benefit the approximately 50,000 residents in its service area.

The site's location on a prominent intersection inspired a community-serving and neighborhood-scale design solution. The goal of the project was to create a non-institutional, family-oriented branch library, so Cy Lemmon designed the building to be as residential in character as possible. This was achieved with a gently sloped gable roof and generous glazing and windows throughout. Wood beams and a shake roof also connected the library to the surrounding neighborhood architecture. The concrete walls received a finish created from a mix of plaster textured with sand and Wai'anae sandstone. The wood beams and shake roof enhance the open design. The project pioneered the use of Wai'anae sandstone on the exterior walls, and the firm used the material again in several notable projects, including Sinclair Library and the University of Hawai'i at Mānoa.

Lemmon designed several cast-stone decorations fabricated by artist Mario Valdastri, who had been casting stone in Honolulu since 1926. He came to Hawai'i from California to work on panels at the Honolulu Academy of Arts. Valdastri created two significant pieces for the library. Adjacent to the main library entrance is a large cast-stone screen representing a Hawaiian canoe surrounded by wave motifs. The second, a cast-stone sign in a sandstone pier that reads, "Library of Hawai'i Waikīkī-Kapahulu Branch," sits along the front walkway.

The building interior offers spacious open areas with tall windows that rise to the roof gables at each end, providing an abundance of natural light. An outdoor reading area further provides the connection of the building interior to the exterior. The Waikīkī-Kapahulu Library remains relatively unchanged to this day and is a celebration of modern design and Hawai'i's climate, community, and culture. •

PROJECT CREDITS

CLIENT

Hawaii State Public Library System

ARCHITECT

Lemmon & Freeth

CHURCHES OF HAWAI'I

COMPLETED **1951–1963**

Completed in 1951, St. Mark's Episcopal Church selected Lemmon & Freeth for what was the first of many religious commissions for the firm.

Paul Jones joined Lemmon, Freeth & Haines in 1955 and became a partner a year later. Jones became known as the firm's "church architect," designing some 50 church projects of differing denominations throughout Hawai'i in the 1950s and 1960s. Jones's church designs were distinctly modern. In a 1965 article in the Honolulu Advertiser about using modern architecture in church design, Jones was quoted,

In 1964, the Honolulu Chapter of the AIA selected 11 O'ahu churches to illustrate O'ahu church construction of architectural significance. These included four designed by Lemmon, Freeth, Haines & Jones: the First Presbyterian Church, the Wesley Methodist Church, Church of the Holy Nativity's Youth Center, and the Kilohana Methodist Church. Paul Jones spoke on "New Visions and Tasks for Church Builders" at a large conference on church architecture, held in Honolulu in 1966.

> *"We are in a changing society that does not define what church functions are. The church today takes on different meanings than the traditional church. Now stronger emphasis as a moving force in secular life is important to the church. It wants to enter into the life of the city, not shut itself off. There's been a lot of deep thinking and bold departures in religious thought. Architecture reflects this."*

The First Presbyterian Church in Honolulu, dedicated on November 26, 1961, is considered one of Paul Jones's finest designs and one of the projects that led to his designation as a Fellow of the American Institute of Architects In 1986. The building was located in a very tight urban site and was the first church in Hawai'i with an underground parking lot. The church embodies a unique pattern of interlacing plastered steel frames that incorporate detailed

lighting fixtures at each intersection. One side of the sanctuary was glazed to provide an intimate view of an enclosed tropical garden. An illuminated 70-foot-high campanile spire marks the front entry on Ke'eaumoku street. The sanctuary employed the use of lava rock, which helped to cut out noise from the adjacent streets.

The Kahuku Methodist church, dedicated May 2, 1965, is also modern in concept, but is so simple that it was built over 100 weekends by the 60-member congregation, with the help of family and friends of various religions. To make this possible, a simple detailing system with a minimum of heavy structural materials and complicated connections evolved during the design and local materials were utilized where possible. Jones described the concept based on an old building tradition of providing a simple shelter with little in the way of walls. The church has a narrow flat roof with steeply sloped sides of redwood board-and-batten and a six-foot-high tile base. Ventilation was provided by baffles and eave overhangs, eliminating the need for extensive glazing.

The modern Aldersgate Methodist Church utilized a unique ventilation system crafted to meet the complex problems of the highly urbanized Kalihi location. Jones designed the church as well as the adjacent education building.

The modern-style Kailua Community Methodist Church includes four murals created by famed artist Jean Charlot that were executed in ceramics by Claude Horan. The emblematic three-sided bell tower at the church entrance encases carillon chimes. The project made careful use of the topography and included rock walls, and an open lanai and rainbow windows at the exterior walls.

Beautiful in their own right, this collection of mid-century churches is made more important by their relationship to each other. They explore light, space, and material in both bold and delicate ways. Together, these structures provide a unique window into Hawai'i's history and sit at the intersection of architecture, religion, modernism, and sacred space. •

PROJECT CREDITS

ARCHITECT

Lemmon & Freeth; Lemmon, Freeth & Haines; Lemmon, Freeth, Haines & Jones

SINGLE-FAMILY RESIDENCES

COMPLETED **1948–1965**

Single family residential design was a large component of the firm's work in its first few decades, and many islanders entrusted the firm for residential work throughout the state.

The firm designed more than 150 single-family houses between 1948 and 1965 and numerous additions and alterations of existing homes. The mid-century residential architecture of the firm was suited for integrating local climate, landscape, and lifestyle. The firm approached the design challenges of addressing weather, heat, and humidity by incorporating air flow and passive temperature control. Much of the firm's residential work aimed to achieve flexible floor plans, often integrating sliding doors that allowed for the opening and closing of various rooms, or in some cases, the entire home. Kitchen space was typically divided with built-in features to provide functionality and designed to be as efficient as possible.

The firm also designed multiple residential housing projects such as the 90-unit Kāne'ohe Peninsula subdivision, created in 1952. The designs combined the casualness of seashore living with modern facilities for efficient homemaking. Two- and three-bedroom options were available, with variations on each for individuality. The interior utilized an open concept with the kitchen integrated into the living space.

As the firm grew over the decades, its combined projects evolved to include commercial, civic, and multi-unit residential buildings. Over time, the single-family projects became a smaller percentage of the firm's overall workload, but the residential projects they designed in the following decades continued to develop the design principles that would form the firm's foundation: understanding the climate conditions, listening to the client needs, and integrating modern design to have style and grace. ▪

CYRIL LEMMON RESIDENCE

Located in the Waialae-Kāhala area, the design angled the home on the plot to utilize the hillside backdrop for maximum privacy, charm, and outdoor living. The U-shaped plan allowed for privacy from the neighbors and featured a lovely vista across the golf course fairway. The design included lava rock, gnarled posts, shoji-type paneling in cosmopolitan flavor, with wood interior walls, brick fireplace, and ceramic lighting fixtures.

CROCKETT RESIDENCE

The Crockett residence was one of the firm's initial private residential projects. The design took full advantage of the waterfront location with views of the ocean, surf, and sky, and a flexible layout that provided areas for entertaining and daily family living.

CROWELL RESIDENCE

Perched on the hillside above ʻĀina Haina, this 1955 home's design allows views of the valley below and provides a windbreak for the lanai located against the hillside. Sliding doors allow the interior living areas to be open as one large space or be closed to offer smaller private rooms as needed.

PROJECT CREDITS

ARCHITECT
Lemmon & Freeth; Lemmon, Freeth & Haines; Lemmon, Freeth, Haines & Jones

Photo: Andrea Brizzi

HAWAI'I STATE CAPITOL BUILDING

COMPLETED

1969

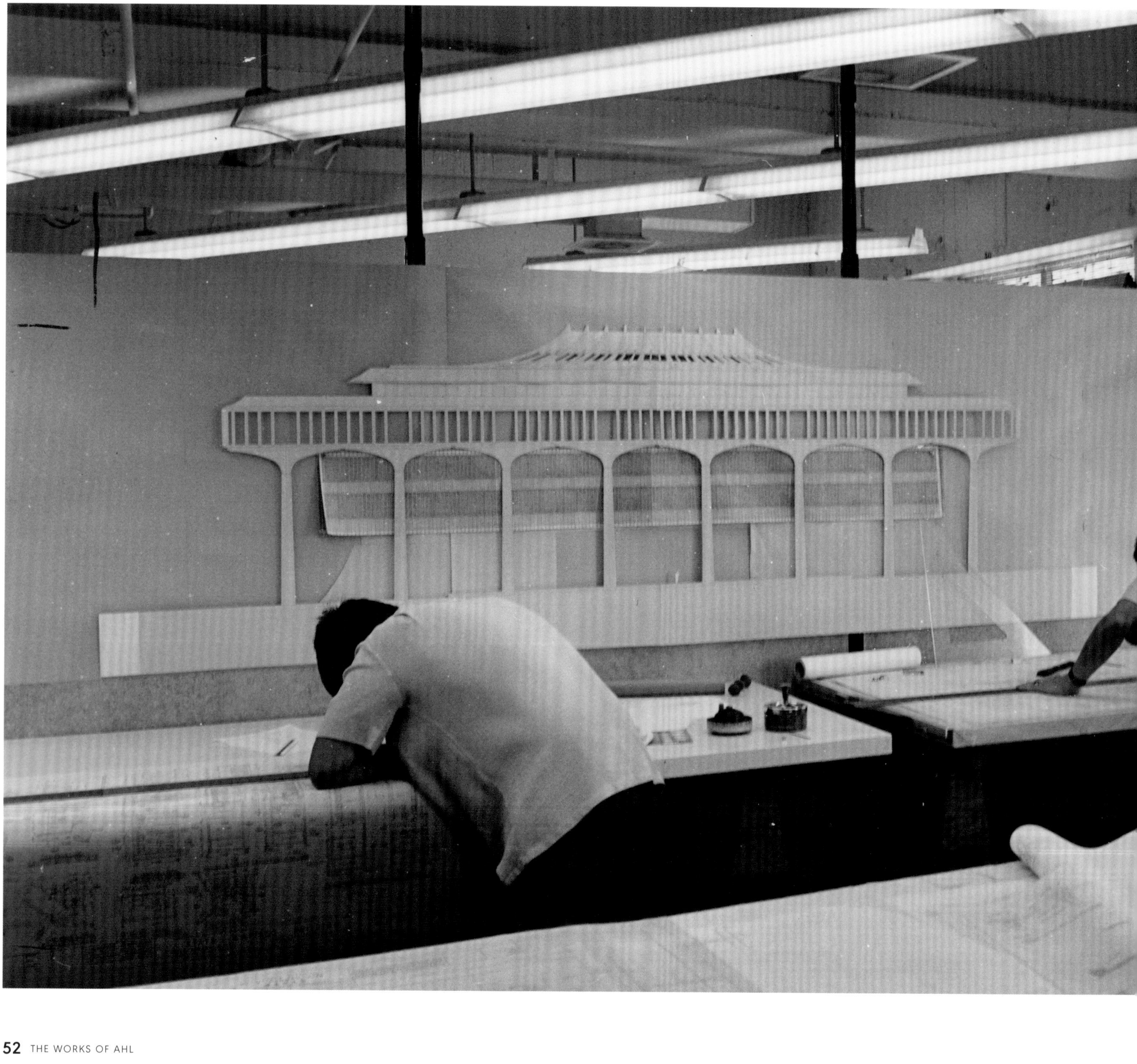

After nearly a decade of design and planning, construction on the iconic Hawai'i State Capitol building commenced in 1965. AHL, and their joint venture team of Belt, Lemmon & Lo, worked with a talented team of men and women to actualize visions for an open-air, modernist government building that was the first of its kind.

The Capitol was designed in the Bauhaus style of "Hawaiian International Architecture" and was inspired by Hawai'i's natural surroundings. In the words of Governor John A. Burns at the 1969 dedication ceremony, the lack of doors at the State Capitol's grand entrances represent "the open sea, open sky, the open doorway, open arms, and open hearts" that have become representative of Hawai'i's warm, welcoming aloha spirit. The design team abandoned the classic rotunda featured in most capitol buildings for a central atrium that exposes the sky; inviting sun, tradewinds, and the occasional rainbow into the lofty, emblematic space. This open-air design intentionally relinquished the atrium to eliminate separation from the "vast inner court from the heavens and from the same eternal stars which guided the first voyagers to the primeval beauty of these shores." Other symbolic elements include eight grandiose, 60-foot-high columns to represent palm trees and Hawai'i's eight main islands while a shallow, exterior reflecting pool emulates the Pacific Ocean. Cone-shaped legislative chambers pay homage to our origins— the volcanoes that formed the Hawaiian Islands. The number four bears heavy significance in many design features as well, representing Hawai'i's four counties and four major Hawaiian gods, *Kūkā'ilimoku*, *Kāne*, *Lono*, and *Kanaloa*. Each chamber has four windows and is accessible through one of four doorways. Four pillars mark interior and exterior corners of the fourth floor, and four prominent kukui trees enliven the open-air courtyard.

"THE LACK OF DOORS AT THE STATE CAPITOL'S GRAND ENTRANCES REPRESENT 'THE OPEN SEA, OPEN SKY, THE OPEN DOORWAY, OPEN ARMS, AND OPEN HEARTS' THAT HAVE BECOME REPRESENTATIVE OF HAWAI'I'S WARM, WELCOMING ALOHA SPIRIT..."

- Governor John A. Burns

Photo: Andrea Brizzi

The Hawai'i State Capitol was completed in 1969 and symbolized natural beauty while breaking many boundaries of architectural design both in Hawai'i and across the United States. Of this iconic and defining project, AHL founder, Cy Lemmon said,

> *"It was felt that the design should be a symbol of our geographical location, our way of life, and environment. A great deal of research was made into Hawaiian history, legends and customs. We felt something which was simple and dignified but could still retain the monumental character and freshness of the Hawaiian concept was what we were after. Most architects only have the opportunity to come in at one stage along the way in a building like this. We've been with it all the way. The fact that we have the chance to develop a State Capitol makes us doubly fortunate."*

The Hawai'i State Capitol celebrated its 50th anniversary in 2019 with a heartfelt commemoration and has been listed on the National Register of Historic Places since 1979. To this day, it remains the only modernist state capitol in the nation. •

PROJECT CREDITS

CLIENT
City & County of Honolulu

ARCHITECT
John Carl Warnecke and Associates in partnership with Belt, Lemmon & Lo Architects Engineers

CONTRACTOR
Reed & Martin, Inc.

STRUCTURAL/CIVIL ENGINEER
Belt, Lemmon & Lo Architects Engineers

DESIGN PRINCIPLES

› Highly symbolic

› Replaced 'Iolani Palace, the former capitol building

› Pushed design boundaries in Hawai'i and as an institutional building

› AHL continues ongoing maintenance and repairs

Photo: Andrea Brizzi

HEAD

DIAMOND HEAD APARTMENTS

DIAMOND HEAD SURF, GARDENS, ALI'I, LANAI, GREGG APARTMENTS, MANOR, LEILANI

COMPLETED

1959–1964

DIAMOND HEAD MANOR
SPACIOUS 2-BEDROOM, 1½-BATH, GARDEN APARTMENTS
PRIVATE ENTRANCE
AMPLE PARKING
RENTAL FROM 195 PER MONTH
ALL-ELECTRIC LIVING
RENTAL AGENT: COOKE TRUST COMPANY PHONE 501-607
OR
SEE MANAGER, APT. 101, DIAMOND HEAD GARDENS

During World War II, Hawai'i experienced a severe housing shortage. Following the war, the shortage continued with the return of service members and the addition of many newcomers.

The lack of housing within the urban core spawned the development of many new residential subdivisions, as apartment buildings replaced single-family houses. Beach houses and bungalows punctuated Waikīkī before the war, after walk-up apartments began to appear around Honolulu.

The apartment buildings usually had a rectangular or L-shaped footprint and were one to four stories in height with single-story units. Materials often included concrete block, black lava rock, brown basalt, sandstone, and other natural and local materials. Parking was usually to one side, but by the 1960s, it was often at ground level underneath the elevated building.

In 1953 Hawai'i lawmakers authorized cooperative (co-op) land tenure, as land prices were continually increasing. For a co-op apartment, the developer would form a non-profit corporation that would own the building as well as legal control of the land. The developer obtained commitments and partial financing from persons who purchased shares in the non-profit, which allowed the developer to secure the funding with which to construct the building. The co-op process benefited the tenants, as it allowed individuals to purchase rather than rent an apartment, and also helped real estate developers financially.

BEACH HOUSES AND BUNGALOWS PUNCTUATED WAIKĪKĪ BEFORE THE WAR, AFTER WALK-UP APARTMENTS BEGAN TO APPEAR AROUND HONOLULU.

DIAMOND HEAD SURF

Colorful ceramics were produced by Ceramics Hawaii for the exterior and swimming pool area.

DIAMOND HEAD GARDENS

The buildings had ceramic panels in bold stripes and used shadow block (textured block cast with depressions to form relief patterns) in accent color panels against the off-white background of surrounding masonry.

DIAMOND HEAD LANAI

Lemmon, Freeth, Haines & Jones placed the one- and two-bedroom units in staggering and cascading boxes to accommodate the irregular lot shape. The 30 two-bedroom units, arranged in a three-story concrete block structure, were broken into single and double units widths to avoid the massive scale of many concrete structures.

GREGG APARTMENTS

Design specifications called for economic concrete block used in unique ways to develop a desired sculptural quality, as illustrated by the 16-foot-deep stairway grillwork.

Lemmon, Freeth, Haines & Jones designed seven apartment buildings at Pualei Circle at the foot of Diamond Head, including the Diamond Head Surf (completed 1959), Diamond Head Gardens (1960), Diamond Head Ali'i (1960), Diamond Head Manor (1962), Diamond Head Lanai (1963), Diamond Head Leilani (1963), and the Gregg Apartments (1964).

The Diamond Head Gardens (42 units), Diamond Head Surf (40 units), and Diamond Head Ali'i (54 units) projects were co-ops and designed by Frank Haines. The Diamond Head Lanai (30 units), Diamond Head Manor (18 units), and Diamond Head Leilani (57 units) were rental units and designed by Joe Farrell. Farrell also designed The Gregg Apartments (30 units) as condominiums. The concept for the apartment buildings was to provide luxury *kama'aina* living at a moderate cost. Features included the proximity to Waikīkī and Kapi'olani Park, beaches, the lush Diamond Head area, and the private and quiet living.

The apartment buildings had various combinations of studio, one-bedroom, and two-bedroom units, and were two, three, or four stories in height, and were of concrete or concrete block construction. Amenities typically comprised a swimming pool, barbeque and exterior lounging areas, and one parking space per unit.

Five of these apartments were the only low-rise apartments given recognition of Honor Awards by the Hawaii Chapter of the AIA; in 1960, the Diamond Head Gardens, Diamond Head Ali'i, and Diamond Head Surf; in 1963, the Diamond Head Lanai; and in 1966 the Gregg Apartments. •

PROJECT CREDITS

ARCHITECT
Lemmon, Freeth, Haines & Jones

HOUSE & SCHOOL BUILDING PROTOTYPES

COMPLETED **1963**

In the 1960s, the American Samoa government implemented a new method for teaching students: television programming.

They recognized that they were not able to provide enough English-speaking teachers, particularly in rural areas, to educate at the level that was needed, so they began a program of using televised instruction in the classrooms. With electrical upgrades to rural schools, the students could watch recorded learning programs. A large transmitter was built on top of Mt. Alava above the capital city of Pago Pago to transmit to the school televisions. With no road to the site, a helicopter delivered the prefabricated materials for the transmitter and building. Additionally, the government built a television studio in Pago Pago to record the instructional programs.

In 1962, Lemmon, Freeth, Haines & Jones were hired by the American Samoan government to design a prototype house and a prototype school building. The island climate is hot, humid, and rainy, and breezes are cherished. The open-lashed Samoan fale structure provided the basis for the resulting designs. Paul Jones served as architect in charge of the project. He stated, "The design concept for all buildings was the same, and if one were to select a title for the style, it would probably be something like *palagi fale* (Caucasian person)." The designs took into account not only the climatic conditions of Samoa, which eliminates walls to the greatest extent possible,

ONE BEDROOM UNIT

but also the ethnic and historical background of the logic, which resulted in the indigenous architecture of the Samoan fale. As a result, most of the buildings are predominantly roof.

The buildings had few walls, featuring screened areas where plaited coconut palm mats or canvas panels could roll down for protection against the elements. The pre-cast concrete columns were set in concrete slabs. The roof was steeply pitched and clad with shingles and had five-foot eaves. The shingles for the roofs were from Washington state. The government blasted a 50-foot-deep channel to provide a means of shipping the construction materials to build the structures from the main island of Tutuila to the three outlying islands, Aunuu, Swains Island, and Manua. Each Chief had full title to all property in their village and had to deed land to the government, and each village's Chief gave the full title to the ground for the school in a ceremonial function called a "Fono."

In all, the American Samoa government constructed 138 school buildings and 73 houses for teachers, meaning that for the first time, there were high school facilities available for every elementary school child. Previously only about one in three graduates of elementary schools attended high school due to the lack of buildings and teachers. The new structures included televisions, where children were seated to watch the learning programs.

AHL Senior Associate and Historic Architect Katie Stephens notes that in 2013,

> *"When I was involved in a project to survey all public school buildings in the US Territories, including America Samoa, I saw these 1960s AHL-designed fale structures. They are still in use, and although jalousies or louvers fill in most open sides, they continue to impart a wonderful culturally-influenced design compared with the modern style buildings around them."* •

PROJECT CREDITS

CLIENT

US Territory of American Samoa

ARCHITECT

Lemmon, Freeth, Haines & Jones

FIRST FEDERAL SAVINGS AND LOAN & FIRST HAWAIIAN BANK

COMPLETED

1965 First Federal Savings & Loan / **1981** First Hawaiian Bank Hale'iwa

During the mid-1960s, Lemmon, Freeth, Haines & Jones began experimenting with new architectural vocabularies for its projects.

Architecture for public and civic buildings was moving toward Brutalism as a response to large-scale changes in technology and society. These innovative designs included unfinished surfaces, straight lines, organic shapes, and heavy-looking materials.

First Federal's 4,440-square-foot office exterior incorporated this new design aesthetic that featured exposed cast-in-place concrete with dynamic cantilevered forms and trellises for shade, protection, and landscaping. The interiors featured a central open space with a bridge-like pass-over at the second level. The building was well received by the community and won the 1969 Honor Award from the Hawaii Chapter American Institute of Architects.

First Federal Savings & Loan envisioned its new Makiki Branch as small in size, but significant in its statement of presence as a preeminent local financial institution. With the construction of the First Federal Savings & Loan, the firm was able to test new design aesthetics and techniques that would later on be applied to a number projects around the island, including the Federal Building Complex.

Twenty years after designing the First Federal Savings & Loan, Architects Hawaii was asked to design another financial institution. First Hawaiian Bank Hale'iwa had long been a prominent part of the community and the bank was looking to expand its 800-square-foot location. At the time, the bank wisely decided to build on a completely different site and donate the local landmark to the town. The old building was used as a model for the overall character of the new structure, utilizing warm materials, traditional roof forms, and residential scale to retain the old building's sense of comfort and informality.

Architects Hawaii's design approach focused on a strong roof form, "floating" above the interior spaces. Deep eaves supplied shade for the interior spaces and reduced energy costs. The building's exposed aggregate concrete base provided a sturdy connection with the ground, and the pitched roof form allowed for the creation of a grand central space for the interior. The "floating" roof was visually separated from its base by a band of glazing that wrapped around the building. Historic photos of the old branch reinforce the bank's enduring presence in the Hale'iwa community.

First Hawaiian Bank's new Hale'iwa Branch conveys community and understated elegance in its historical town context. It was completed in late 1981 and received an Award of Excellence in Architecture from the Hawaii Society AIA and The Hawai'i Architectural Arts Award from Hawai'i's State Foundation on Culture and the Arts. •

PROJECT CREDITS

CLIENT
First Federal Savings & Loan
First Hawaiian Bank

ARCHITECT
Lemmon, Freeth, Haines & Jones

CONTRACTOR
Universal Construction

AWARDS

- AIA Honolulu Chapter Award of Merit, 1989
- City & County of Honolulu Project of the Year Award, Honorable Mention, 1988

1962–1972

THE RISE OF DOWNTOWN

By the early 1960s, the populations of the state and firm were growing. With nearly 50 staff members, the firm made a strategic move to relocate downtown where an increasing number of AHL's clients were now located. The new office was on the 15th floor of their newly designed First Hawaiian Bank Tower in downtown Honolulu. First Hawaiian Bank was a major client of the firm and in 1959 First Hawaiian selected AHL to design their new Downtown office tower, which at the height of 18 stories succeeded the ten-story Aloha Tower as Hawai'i's tallest building.

From that day, AHL would play a major role in the planning and design of Downtown Honolulu. Cy realized gaining a reputation for successfully completing large, complex projects like First Hawaiian was a key element in his vision for the firm; not just as architects but additionally demonstrating the firm's commitment to the growth of Downtown Honolulu and the State Capitol District.

This clear vision is clearly exhibited in their design of one of AHL's and the State's more iconic and important projects, the Hawai'i State Capitol building. As the country's newest state, Hawai'i's unique culture and location demanded a new and modern design response that the firm delivered. The success of the First Hawaiian Tower and the State Capitol Building solidified AHL's position as one of the leading design firms in the state, ultimately securing other major projects including the Kona Surf Resort, Hawai'i's largest building construction project to date, the US Federal Building and Courthouse Complex, and AHL's future home, the Pacific Trade Center.

FIRST NATIONAL BANK & FIRST HAWAIIAN BANK TOWER

COMPLETED **1962**

The 1950s began with Honolulu's historic retail center in Downtown. By the end of the decade, retail's "center of gravity" had shifted.

With the opening of America's largest shopping mall in 1959, Ala Moana Shopping Center accelerated the growth of personal automobile transportation throughout O'ahu. Ala Moana's central location between Downtown and Waikīkī shifted O'ahu's retail core toward the east, enabling greater focus on Downtown's professional and office development moving forward.

Landlocked between Chinatown to the west and the State Capitol District to the east, Honolulu's government and civic leaders considered many means of providing more urban, high-density development opportunities in the nascent State. Bishop National Bank of Hawai'i (renamed to First Hawaiian Bank in 1969) engaged Lemmon, Freeth, Haines & Jones in 1959 to design their modernist Downtown office building, envisioned as matching Aloha Tower's ten-story height. Planning and design discussions resulted in the City's approval for Bishop National Bank of Hawaii's office building well exceeding Aloha Tower's height at 18 stories, and Downtown Honolulu's building boom was erupted.

Bishop National Bank of Hawaii's 225-foot office tower was Hawai'i's first modern high-rise. The tower, set in a landscaped sidewalk plaza, was equipped with high-speed elevators, drive-in tellers, and a multi-level parking garage with a service station. The concrete tower structure set a precedent in Hawai'i, utilizing highly efficient driven piles into Downtown's deep subterranean coral shelf to support the tower; a practice later applied on numerous other Downtown high-rises yet to come.

Bishop National Bank of Hawaii had long inhabited the historic low-rise Damon Building. The new modern tower design respected the Damon Building's façade. It maintained the bank's downtown branch therein, while preserving open space at the pedestrian level through tower setbacks along Bishop Street and King Street. The tower's modern design expressed functionality and order while featuring extensive city view. The top-floor penthouse featured executive meeting and dining facilities for 45 persons, a president's room displaying historical items from the bank's opening in 1858, and guestroom accommodations.

With the Hawai'i State Capitol under construction concurrent with the Bishop National Bank of Hawaii Tower, Lemmon, Freeth, Haines & Jones founder CY Lemmon chose to relocate the firm's offices from Kapi'olani Boulevard's Kenrock Building to the new Bishop National Bank of Hawaii Tower. Lemmon, Freeth, Haines & Jones moved to the 15th Floor in 1963, and the firm has remained in Downtown Honolulu thereafter. The office moved into its newer Bishop Street office high-rises, then to American Savings Bank Tower in the 1970s, and its present location in Pacific Guardian Center in 2012.

Over the years, high-rise tower design has been a core specialty of the firm. From Bishop National Bank of Hawaii in 1959 to the present, AHL has carried out over 30 high-rise projects, including offices, apartments, hotels and timeshares, and hospitals, in Hawai'i, the Pacific, and Asia.

Although digital work stations have replaced the drawing board desks of decades past, AHL's office environments have always supported a modern mentality emphasizing open, light-filled spaces that are functional, flexible, and beautiful. •

PROJECT CREDITS

CLIENT

Bishop National Bank Hawaii

ARCHITECT

Lemmon, Freeth, Haines & Jones

MARCO POLO

COMPLETED **1971**

When the 36-story Marco Polo commenced its sales program in December 1969, the tower was Hawai'i's most significant residential condominium. From its completion in 1971 to the age of newer, taller towers in the 1980s, the Marco Polo was Hawai'i's tallest high-rise residential building.

The Marco Polo's unique location fronting on the Ala Wai Canal provided panoramic views from Mānoa Vally to Diamond Head and Waikīkī. Its uniquely expansive, urban site enabled generous amenity areas for 567 residential units. While luxury hotels and low-rise residences were commonplace by the late 1960s, the Marco Polo set a new standard for high-rise luxury living environments in Hawai'i.

The design of the Marco Polo began in 1968 as the City's new Comprehensive Zoning Code came into effect, and the Marco Polo was the first planned-unit-development built under the new code.

The General Contractor, Alaska-based Reed & Martin Inc., teamed well with Lemmon, Freeth, Haines & Jones after having worked together successfully on the Hawai'i State Capitol from 1965 through 1969. Reed & Martin Inc. took the roles of both developer and contractor for Marco Polo and subsequently brought on the State Capitol architectural team of Lemmon, Freeth, Haines & Jones; John Carl Warnecke; and Walter K. Iagawa & Associates to complete the design.

The Marco Polo's distinctive S-shaped curvilinear design was well received. As noted in Honolulu publications, Marco Polo was "Hawai'i's newest and most prestigious condominium" offering "a study in luxury...

and convenience." Units varied from studios and one- and two-bedrooms to three-bedroom two-story penthouses on the 35th and 36th floors.

Apartment features incorporated wall-to-wall carpeting, a full range of appliances including washer, dryer, dishwasher, double-track drapery, individually controlled air conditioning units, and master TV antennas. Lush landscaping, generous lobby, and lounge are among the featured common facilities. Specialty features included a gourmet shop and restaurant, cocktail lounge, meeting-recreation rooms, swimming pool, tennis and paddle tennis courts, golf driving range, putting green, volleyball area, and men's and women's saunas.

The elegant and timeless Marco Polo continues to be a beautiful addition to the Honolulu skyline and an exemplar of mid-century modern architecture.•

PROJECT CREDITS

CLIENT
Reed & Martin Inc.

ARCHITECT
Lemmon, Freeth, Haines & Jones

CONTRACTOR
Reed & Martin Inc.

OAHU COUNTRY CLUB

COMPLETED **1971**

PROJECT CREDITS

CLIENT
Oahu Country Club

ARCHITECT
Lemmon, Freeth, Haines, Jones & Farrell

CONTRACTOR
J.P. Finan

The Oahu Country Club is one of the oldest private country clubs west of the Rockies. From opening day in 1907, the Oahu Country Club has been a premier attraction for Honolulu's golf enthusiasts.

The Oahu Country Club's unique valley location provides inherent golfing challenges, and unparalleled views across the course of O'ahu's mountains, city skyline, and Pacific Ocean seascape. The club's central location and proximity to Downtown Honolulu provide its members and guests with a unique and enjoyable social environment.

Integral with the course, the 1907 Clubhouse took full advantage of the valley site. Upon selection of Lemmon, Freeth, Haines, Jones & Farrell as the architect for the new Clubhouse expansion, the design team faced the challenge of constructing an entirely new building in the same location as the existing building while maintaining the Club's full operation during demolition and replacement phases.

Lemmon, Freeth, Haines, Jones & Farrell's overall design approach focused on reflecting and celebrating the 1907 Clubhouse with its quiet architecture featuring traditional pitched roofs and lava rock walls. The expanded program enabled the new larger structure to achieve a stature and scale more in harmony with its dramatic natural surroundings.

The execution challenge was met by carefully planning five stages of construction. The first stage of construction demolished the original Clubhouse's main exterior lanai and related entry, keeping dining and kitchen areas operational while constructing roughly half of the new renovation. Club operations then moved into the new facility. Next, demolition of the remainder of the original Clubhouse occurred, completing the renovation. New additions included a Pro Shop in a separate building across from a welcoming new porte-cochere. Construction took place over 16 months with the new Clubhouse facility opening on July 31, 1970.

The new Clubhouse marks a simple, strong, and sophisticated interior experience surrounded by a positive presence in natural surroundings. Double-pitched roof forms, flat ceilings transitioning to generous roof overhangs, and floor-to-ceiling glass areas carry the eye from the inside out. Neutral earth tones combine with lava rock, further blending interior spaces with the outdoors. Lemmon, Freeth, Haines, Jones & Farrell's new Clubhouse for Oahu Country Club seamlessly blends history, architecture, nature, and experience to create a uniquely Hawaiian sense of place. •

ʻIOLANI SCHOOL

LIBRARY AND GYMNASIUM

COMPLETED

1967 'Iolani Library - Learning Center **/ 1960** 'Iolani Gymnasium and Athletic Facilities

Hawai'i's public education system was established in 1840 by King Kamehameha III. The name '*Iolani* (heavenly hawk) honors the late King Kamehameha IV, born Alexander Liholiho 'Iolani.

In 1862 Kamehameha IV, a devout member of the Church of England, established the Hawaiian Reformed Catholic Church, which became known as the Anglican Church of Hawai'i, and in 1863 the St. Alban's College for Boys was established in Pauoa Valley in Honolulu.

As the opportunities expansion and evolution of education efforts grew throughout the islands, St. Alban's was moved to Nu'uanu Valley, intending it for students of full or part Hawaiian descent, under the new name of "'Iolani College." The name *'Iolani* (heavenly hawk) honors the late King Kamehameha IV, born Alexander Liholiho'Iolani.

In 1953 'Iolani School moved to its present Ala Wai site. Starting with a few wartime wooden buildings, the school embarked on realizing its vision in the mid-1960s. They entrusted Lemmon, Freeth, Haines & Jones as architects for the first major new buildings, which established the campus core and were surrounded by exterior open space.

The designers faced challenges with the site restrictions and those limitations partially determined the configuration of the buildings.

The new multi-level Library-Learning Center contained 30,000 volumes; 100 carrels; a microfilm booth; seminar room and offices; extensive audio-visual facilities; and a 154 seat auditorium for assemblies, student performances, and class sessions. Other facilities included language and audio-visual labs, offices, conference rooms, special classrooms, and a faculty lounge.

A large lanai was provided below the library complex for school and social functions, serving as a space for students to gather, socialize, and study. Although the school has replaced the original library building, the library lanai remains and has become an iconic space for 'Iolani School, endearingly nicknamed, "Senior Benches." The area maintains a first-day-of-school tradition for the incoming senior class to claim the best bench on the lanai.

The new full athletic courtyard at 'Iolani School featured a gymnasium building, swimming pool, locker rooms, tennis courts, a 440-yard track, and a baseball field. The two-story gymnasium building included a full second-story basketball court, physical fitness rooms on both floors, and athletic staff offices on the ground floor. Detailed wind studies were conducted to best orient the building for trade-wind access. Second-floor spaces featured motorized jalousies for maximum ventilation with vertical redwood baffles to minimize direct sunlight.

At the time, the new Upper School two-story, ten-classroom buildings were the only air-conditioned classrooms on the campus. Precast vertical baffles at window openings provided sun control. The Lower School added 15 classrooms plus a 5,000-volume library with audio-visual and music appreciation facilities, and the adjoining pre-school received alterations and modifications.

In 1979 'Iolani School became co-educational, ending its all-male enrollment policy, offering a standard college preparatory curriculum as a foundation for every student. •

PROJECT CREDITS

CLIENT
'Iolani School

ARCHITECT
Lemmon, Freeth, Haines, Jones & Farrell

CONTRACTOR
S & M Sakamoto

PRINCE JONAH KŪHIŌ KALANIANAʻOLE FEDERAL BUILDING

COMPLETED

1977

The 1950s were an exuberant time for Hawai'i with the anticipation of pending Statehood. Planning and design discussions focused on expressing Hawai'i's emergence as the newest state in America, by weaving modern design together with unique lifestyle and tropical climate.

As an island state with a consequential cost of shipping, Hawai'i's construction technology and resultant design palette focused heavily on indigenous materials, with reinforced concrete being the preferred structural and exterior framing element for more significant buildings and various large complexes.

Design on the Honolulu Federal Building Complex began shortly after Hawai'i's Statehood of August 21, 1959. Located a short walk from downtown and the new Hawai'i State Capitol, the Federal Building complex would be one of Hawai'i's most significant buildings to date.

In the 1950s, high-rises were seen by many as signs of progress and expressions of significance. Shortly before Statehood, the firm designed First Hawaiian Bank's Headquarters, which at 17 stories became Hawai'i's tallest building. The Downtown area in this nascent state experienced a surge of high-rise growth, and the Federal Government's General Services Administration envisioned the new Honolulu Federal Complex as a high-rise, perhaps Hawai'i's tallest.

Having only recently completed the Hawai'i State Capitol, the firm was deeply involved in the master planning of the Hawai'i Capitol Special District. Planning guidelines for the District included no structure being taller than the Hawai'i State Capitol, which has a cornice height of 64.5 feet, and a roof height of 91 feet. The Hawai'i State Capitol was naturally the heart of the District. The firm felt strongly that the Federal Building site, although not in the official District, was its conceptual *makai* (ocean) anchor.

APPLYING THIS PHILOSOPHY INVOLVED TWO MAJOR LINES OF THOUGHT; CONSIDERATION OF THE PEDESTRIAN SCALE AND HUMAN EXPERIENCE IN VISITING AND INHABITING THIS EXTREMELY LARGE COMPLEX.

Firm principals took the initiative to meet with appropriately high-level GSA individuals and push their case for a low-rise complex, with an interior courtyard and a garden terrace. They felt this design would be a better neighbor in Honolulu's civic center and more appropriate to Hawai'i. They expressed that there will undoubtedly be many high-rises from Downtown to Waikīkī and beyond. This pattern of post-WWII growth was occurring in cities throughout the US and Europe, and the subsequent effect was that the newest high-rises often eclipse previous ones in size, notoriety, and acceptance. Honolulu's State Capitol District is the focal point of development in all directions around urban Honolulu. Hawai'i's planners have ensured the Capitol District's future visual prominence through the enactment of Special District View Channels. As a result, Hawai'i's State Capitol District's generously landscaped open space and low-rise government buildings will remain meaningful and beneficial to residents and visitors long into the future. GSA agreed with this philosophy, and the design proceeded accordingly.

Applying this philosophy involved two critical lines of thought; consideration of the pedestrian scale and the human experience in visiting and inhabiting this vast complex housing roughly 2,500 employees in approximately 90 government agencies. The site design concept focused on "use paths" from surrounding high-density areas considering pedestrians and public transit. The design placed the primary pedestrian entrance on the *mauka* side along Halekauwila Street, generally on axis with anticipated future government buildings leading to the Hawai'i State Capitol. The design concept envisioned the Federal Building Complex as the counterpoint to the State Capitol Building and the *makai* terminus for the State Capitol District.

Designers worked from the multiple use paths to break up the roughly 630,000-square-foot area for the building program with several interrelated forms that step up in scale from the *mauka* (mountain) side of the site to the *makai* (ocean) side. The stepped massing relates to the pedestrian scale within the Capitol District and the larger, more commercial scale along Ala Moana Boulevard and the ocean. The true design goal was to create a building that expressed the Federal Government's support and presence in the newest State of America.

The building mass scales down towards Halekauwila Street, where there is a high volume of pedestrian traffic. The low-rise Courts Building sits in a lush "jewel-box" landscaped setting in front of the more elevated tower of offices at the V-shaped intersection of Ala Moana and Halekauwila Street. The *makai* side of Ala Moana Boulevard is primarily vehicular, hence the higher office massing along this connector from Honolulu's Downtown to Waikīkī. The forms become narrower as the building height increases, providing a variety of floor plate size to accommodate all agencies, large and small. The stairs

and elevator are expressed in large vertical concrete piers that engage the horizontal floor planes at every level. Large glass façades contrast with stalwart masonry and outdoor ground-level courtyards. The interior spaces and exterior grounds of the Federal Building Complex incorporate works from both Hawai'i and US Mainland artists including a large sculptural outdoor feature that highlights the intersection of the building massing.

The complex building massing provides visual interest both from within the facility and from outside surroundings. The design team utilized exposed coral aggregate hand-hammered concrete and split-faced concrete masonry units (CMU) to express Hawai'i's indigenous building palette. Clear sealers rather than paint emphasize this philosophy, a rarity for architecture in Hawai'i at that time.

A historical note: the Federal Complex's original 1960s design program included the Hawai'i Regional Post Office, located in the two broadest ground and second floors. During the completion of construction documents, GSA's consideration of increasing travel to Hawai'i by air over sea prompted the decision to eliminate the Post Office from the Federal Complex's program and relocate it to the Honolulu International Airport. GSA, however, instructed the architects to keep the overall form as is. Shortly after that, GSA selected the firm to redesign the Post Office as a stand-alone building at the newly expanded Honolulu International Airport.

Later during the 1970s, the state selected AHL as architects for the new Hawai'i State Office Building, now named Ke'elikolani State Office Building. Located directly across Halekauwila Street, its low-rise exterior uses a similar exposed aggregate concrete and glass palette yet in a new way and in a new form. •

PROJECT CREDITS

CLIENT

US Government General Services Administration

ARCHITECT

Lemmon & Freeth; Lemmon, Freeth & Haines; Lemmon, Freeth, Haines & Jones

CONTRACTOR

Haas and Haynie Corp.

KONA SURF HOTEL

COMPLETED

1971

WHILE MOST OF THE SURF RESORTS WERE MIDDLE LEVEL AND OF STANDARD CONSTRUCTION, THE PRISTINE, MOSTLY LAVA-COVERED OCEANFRONT SITE AT KONA'S KEAUHOU BAY CRIED FOR A UNIQUE DESIGN.

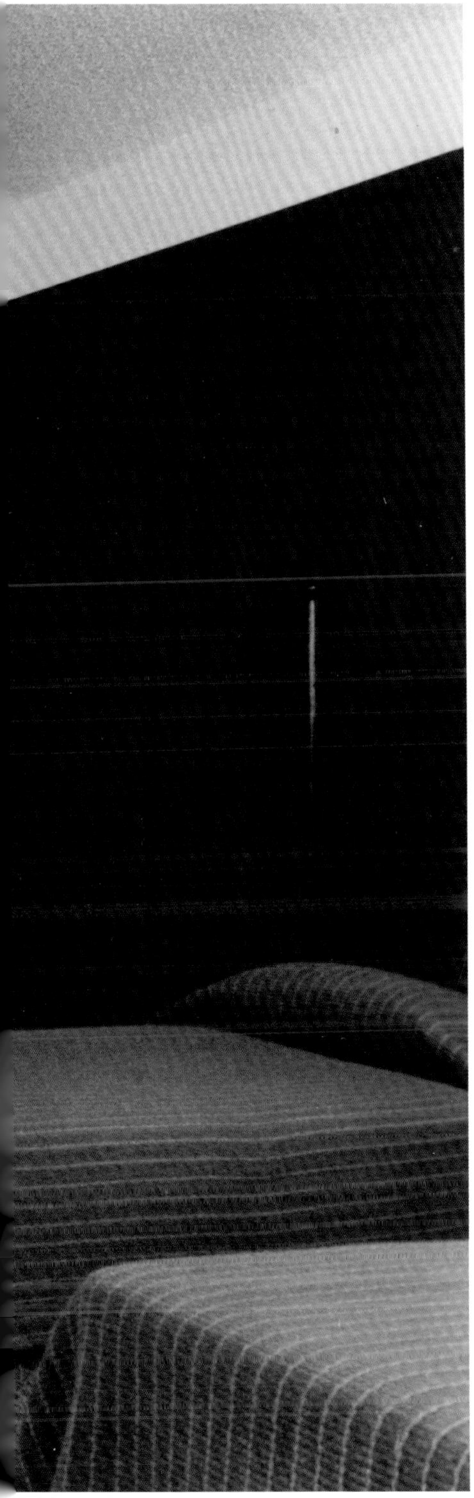

The Kona Surf Hotel was designed in the late 1960s and opened in 1971. Following Lawrence Rockefeller's high-end luxury Big Island Mauna Kea Beach Hotel, which opened in 1965, the Kona Surf played a crucial role in "writing the book" on experiential, integrated neighbor island resort development for Hawai'i's more economically affluent visitors.

By the 1960s, AHL had an established relationship with Hawai'i's major locally owned hotel company, Interisland Resorts. Its CEO was Walter D. (Dudley) Child, who owned the historic Blaisdell Hotel on Fort Street in the 1930s. Child founded Interisland Resorts in Honolulu in the 1940s and later founded Surf Resorts with properties on Kaua'i, Maui, and the Big Island. AHL's Interisland Surf Resort projects included the Naniloa Surf, Kauai Surf, and Kona Surf.

While most of the Surf Resorts were middle level and of standard construction, the pristine, mostly lava-covered oceanfront site at Kona's Keauhou Bay cried for a unique design approach, which the firm proposed. Child enthusiastically endorsed the plan, creating Interisland Resort's "Jewel in the Crown" Surf Resort.

The Kona Surf Hotel was the feature design element in Kamehameha Development's overall master plan for its 14.5-acre oceanfront coastline site, six miles east of historic Kailua Kona. The dominant site characteristic is undulating exotic lava rock outcroppings. AHL's design was driven by the dramatic landforms and seascape. The buildings merged with the rock outcroppings to minimize the site disturbance and preserve the distinctive lava landscape while also providing an authentic visitor experience. They achieved this goal by utilizing guestroom modules combined in a linear sequence, stepping horizontally and vertically to the profile of the site, creating a variety of forms and spaces. Pedestrian circulation, which was

literally through the lava fields, further enhanced the views of the open ocean, coastlines, and mountains. In expressing the site's unique qualities, landscaping was placed selectively within rather than throughout the site, emphasizing its strong lava forms and ocean and mountain vistas beyond.

Building landscape coalesced in all aspects of the resort from the public areas to the amenity zones to produce an iconic project. Modern and refined, a visitor to the Kona Surf Hotel (now the Outrigger Kona Resort & Spa) experiences the enormity of the Big Island and Keauhou Bay. •

PROJECT CREDITS

CLIENT
Kona Pacific Associates (Inter Island Resorts)

ARCHITECT
Lemmon, Freeth, Haines & Jones

CONTRACTOR
Hirano Bros., Ltd.

DESIGN PRINCIPLES

› Guest rooms face ocean, quiet bay, golf course, and mountain slopes in a satisfying display of nature's beauty

› A feeling of spaciousness and unity with the environment

› Respect for the existing site and minimizing the ground disturbance

› A modern "Jewel of the Crown"

1010 WILDER

COMPLETED **1970**

1010 Wilder's highly successful development, designed and constructed in the early 1970s, came about through a Dillingham Land Corporation; Lemmon, Freeth, Haines, Jones & Farrell; and Hawaiian Dredging Construction Company as the general contractor.

Conveniently located close to Downtown Honolulu, the State Capitol District, The Pacific Club, Punahou School, and Ala Moana Park and Shopping Center, 1010 Wilder's quiet, gently sloping site was an ideal residential location for prominent members of the community.

Lemmon, Freeth, Haines, Jones & Farrell's design concept was an 18-story tower, oriented east towards Diamond Head, and offering outstanding views to Honolulu's mountains, ocean, and emerging skyline. Basic plans provided four spacious two-bedroom apartments per floor, each with approximately 1,400-square-feet of interior space plus a 300-square-foot lanai. The tower's distinct sculpted form enabled larger and smaller floor plates, increasing the range of apartment choices for buyers. High ceilings and single-loaded corridors enhanced views and natural fresh air circulation for the apartments.

Anticipated buyer profiles included persons moving from a single-family house desiring customization to the new apartment. Concurrent presale and construction schedules enabled individual buyers a variety of tailored options. Intense architect-general contractor collaboration on design and scheduling delivered a high level of customization while the overall tower shell was constructed simultaneously. The building's shell design included high ceilings and utility location options. 1010 Wilder's completed tower mix includes four, three, two, or only one apartment per floor.

With its distinctive silhouette and prime location, 1010 Wilder has endured as a premier address for Honolulu's *kama'aina* community. •

PROJECT CREDITS

CLIENT
Dillingham Land Corporation

ARCHITECT
Lemmon, Freeth, Haines, Jones & Farrell

CONTRACTOR
Hawaiian Dredging Construction Company

THE BARCLAY

COMPLETED **1969**

Lemmon, Freeth, Haines & Jones designed The Barclay in the mid-1960s. At that time, high-rise residential towers were beginning to appear in response to growing urban population density throughout Honolulu.

The Barclay is designed to be practical and cost-effective while also being visually dynamic. This concrete structure was a significant addition to the rapidly urbanizing Honolulu skyline in the late 1960s. A significant design challenge was the project's site location, immediately adjacent to the elevated H-1 Freeway, which had opened in 1953.

The 17-story, 101-unit tower apartments were designed to reduce the freeway's adverse effects to the property, improve the resident quality of life, and maximize the prized ocean views from apartments. The design concept entailed setting the tower back from the freeway and maintaining a mature banyan tree to screen the highway from lower floor units. Easterly orientation to the trade-winds and a single-loaded corridor plan enabled fresh air ventilation. Apartments were individually angled east toward Diamond Head, reducing direct sun and creating the distinctive saw-toothed building form. The serrated configuration addressed all the design privacy challenges while still providing exceptional views to Diamond Head on the east. The staggered massing was modern and elegant. It allowed The Barclay's façade to transform throughout the day, it's dramatic shadows traveling with the passing cars and the passing sun.

"The Barclay's "state of the art" features included a master TV antenna system, two high-speed Otis elevators, individual apartment electric meters, free-standing washer-dryer combination, manual-cycle control dishwasher, stainless steel disposal, and swimming pool with men's and women's lounges complete with showers."

In 1970, The Barclay received an Honor Award from the Hawaii Chapter of the American Institute of Architects. Well-received by the community, The Barclay received praise in numerous Honolulu publications and is as visually impressive today as it was in 1969. •

PROJECT CREDITS

CLIENT
Loyalty Enterprises Ltd.

ARCHITECT
Lemmon, Freeth, Haines & Jones

CONTRACTOR
Hawaiian Dredging and Construction Co.

HALE KOA HOTEL

COMPLETED **1975**

The Armed Forces Recreation Centers (AFRC) are a chain of resort hotels owned by the US Department of Defense, providing rest and recreation for US Military Service members and their families. The Hale Koa Hotel is the only AFRC inside a military reservation in the United States.

In Hawaiian, *Hale Koa* means "House of the Warrior," a fitting mantle for this military hotel. Designed by AHL in the early 1970s and opened in 1975, it is an affordable first-class hotel and recreational facility that greets over one million visitors each year. AHL's overall design goal focused on maximizing guest experiences by connecting the resort, amenities, and landscape to the property's pristine, 72-acre Waikīkī Beach front lot near Fort DeRussy Military Reservation.

AHL's primary design direction connects Hale Koa Hotel's guestrooms, public amenities, and circulation spaces with its beautifully landscaped site and surroundings. Open, fresh air spaces include the main lobby, front desk, lounges, restaurants and bars, and pool areas. Extensive trellises integrate lounges, dining, and recreation spaces with the site. Sun and shade, natural and artificial lighting, organic colors and materials, and art and graphics together create strong ties to tropical surroundings that recall a luxurious sense of relaxation and ease. Exposed-aggregate concrete angled balconies look out to the lush landscaped site and ocean beyond. As with great nearby hotels, including the Royal Hawaiian and Halekulani Hotel, operations and attention to details reinforce the aloha unique to Hawai'i in beach activities, food and beverage, entertainment, and sports, all services provided by highly personable staff. •

PROJECT CREDITS

CLIENT
Hale Koa Hotel

ARCHITECT
Lemmon, Freeth, Haines, Jones & Farrell

INTERIOR DEISGN
Architects Hawaii Ltd.

CONTRACTOR
Kiewit Pacific Co.

SHRINERS HOSPITAL FOR CHILDREN

COMPLETED **1967**

The concept for Shriners Hospital was a place where children with the crippling effects of polio, clubfoot, and other orthopedic conditions could receive life-changing medical care.

Honolulu Shriners Hospital, the second in their system, was established in a wing of Kauikeolani Children's Hospital in 1923. In 1930, its significantly larger present eight-acre site was conveyed to the Hospital by the prominent Dowsett family. Alterations to the former Dowsett house and several related structures made the complex suitable for hospital use, and Shriners Hospital operated therein for over 35 years.

In the early 1960s, Shriners selected Lemmon, Freeth, Haines & Jones as the architect for the future Honolulu Shriners Hospital. The design brief included the constraint that the 1930s Dowsett Hospital remain operational until the opening of the innovative facility. Lemmon, Freeth, Haines & Jones' Chairman, Cy Lemmon, envisioned the Honolulu Shriners Hospital as a place where infirm and recuperating children could enjoy the playful, childlike wonder and continue their education in an upbeat, friendly atmosphere. Their physical conditions often required long healing and treatment periods, and the Honolulu Shriners Hospital allowed patients to maintain some of the youthful joy of childhood. Hawai'i's natural indoor-outdoor environment was a significant element in Cy Lemmon's conceptualizing a campus plan. The eight-acre site addressed the needs both to keep the existing Hospital in operation while providing a Hawaiian style living environment for children, patients, and all.

Architecturally, the Shriners Hospital evokes Hawaiian culture with a quiet yet striking modernism. The design was a single-story with lush landscaping surrounding the building to promote a strong indoor/outdoor visual and physical connection to promote healing. One's first view of the Hospital from Punahou Street is of a simple, dramatic colonnade framing the entry and low-pitched roof beyond. This set-in expanse of lawn with a grove of Royal Palms creates formal arrival with noble proportions and tasteful restraint.

In 1970, Honolulu Shriners Hospital was awarded the Hawaii Chapter AIA Honor Award for design excellence. •

PROJECT CREDITS

CLIENT
Shriners Hospital

ARCHITECT
Lemmon, Freeth, Haines & Jones

CONTRACTOR
Nordic Construction Ltd.

RAINBOW PROMENADE

COMPLETED **1979**

Japanese tourism in Hawai'i was at a peak in 1980. That year, the New York Times reported that "Japanese investors have now almost every resort hotel on Waikīkī Beach."

Architects Hawaii's client base included numerous Japanese investors who had focused on Hawai'i, including Mitsukoshi, Ltd., an international department store chain headquartered in Tokyo. Purchasing a property at the highly visible corner of Kalākaua and Beachwalk Avenues, Mitsukoshi engaged Architects Hawaii to design a luxury retail building named "Rainbow Promenade" that would also be home to their Waikīkī Mitsukoshi Department Store.

The design for Rainbow Promenade would feature a high-rise commercial development capitalizing on the popularity of the "Ginza-style" vertical shopping centers in Tokyo. Its main intention was to lease to Japanese companies with a presence in Hawai'i .

The design approach capitalized on the unique "V-shaped" site to create visually dynamic form that captured the views from traffic driving easterly into Waikīkī on Kalākaua Avenue. From this approach, the nine-story concrete structure virtually "grew out of" the intersection with elegant curves emphasizing and responding to the corner condition. The first three stories of the design featured glass along its curved perimeter, housing Mitsukoshi's Hawai'i department store, and providing a transparent connection to the exterior vehicular and pedestrian traffic. Ground-floor entries provide access to both the Mitsukoshi store and an atrium with five stories of retail and top-floor penthouse club and restaurant.

RAINBOW PROMENADE

RAINBOW PROM

In addition to the site geometry, the building setbacks also influenced the sculptural building form. A three-story glass water-wall frames the entrance, and an exterior elevator provides customers with an experiential vertical journey through the building. The water-wall entry feature is a Mitsukoshi Corporation trademark used on their other projects. Floating above the glazed entry, the cementitious panel accent enhances the sculptural qualities of the composition and gives the building its distinctive identity. Construction commenced in 1977, and Rainbow Promenade opened in 1979. •

PROJECT CREDITS

CLIENT
Sanpo Land Industrial Inc.

ASSOCIATE ARCHITECT
Architects Hawaii Ltd.

CONTRACTOR
Swinerton & Walberg Co.

1972–2012

A TIME OF TRANSITION

Hawai'i was evolving. By the late 1960s it was clear that the high-rise would become the defining form of Honolulu's built environment and that AHL would be involved in many of the projects that would not only influence the future of Hawai'i but also the Pacific Rim.

One of the most significant projects of this time was the Pacific Trade Center. The owner envisioned the first major high-rise office building in Downtown since First Hawaiian Tower. At 30 stories, the Pacific Trade Center (now American Savings Bank) became the tallest building in Hawai'i. AHL's master plan also saved the site's majestic monkeypod trees from destruction and in the process created one of urban Honolulu's largest and most vibrant green spaces—Tamarind Park. The third floor of the tower, situated within the lush canopy of trees, would be the firm's home for the next 40 years offering a window to the bustling activity of the city and park below.

Many of the AHL's most iconic projects were designed and constructed during this window and the firm enjoyed an expanding sphere of influence working on projects in Hawai'i and throughout the Pacific Rim including: The Grosvenor Center, John A. Burns School of Medicine in Kaka'ako, Federated States of Micronesia Capitol Complex, Palau Capitol, and Kameda Medical Center in Japan.

During this time, AHL formalized its influence in the community by joining the national 1% Program where pro bono time is pledged to benefit local nonprofit projects requiring architectural services. Responding to changing needs of clients, community, and technology, the firm also elected its first female President and CEO. With that barrier shattered, walls, silos, and other conventions would follow.

Photos: Andrea Brizzi

AMERICAN SAVINGS BANK TOWER & PACIFIC GUARDIAN CENTER

COMPLETED

1972 American Savings Bank Tower

COMPLETED

1981 Pacific Guardian Center

Through its two substantial superblock projects along Honolulu's Bishop Street, AHL created Downtown's two largest public plazas, considerable urban spaces that didn't exist previously. AHL's American Savings Bank Tower (ASB) and Pacific Guardian Center (PGC) are contemporary mixed-use superblock tower projects with significant genesis in the history of Honolulu's Downtown.

ASB Tower is located at the *mauka* (mountain) area of Honolulu's Bishop Street, while PGC sits at Bishop Street's *makai* (ocean) side terminus.

From the early 19th century to the present day, Downtown Honolulu's Bishop Street has been the "main street" for Hawai'i's significant corporations, law firms, and other professional and business entities. A short walk from 'Iolani Palace, Washington Place (the Governor's Residence), and the Hawai'i State Capitol, Bishop Street begins *mauka* toward the mountain and terminates at Honolulu Harbor's historic Aloha Tower, which, until the 1950s, was the tallest building in the state.

Bishop Street area has long been home to many of Hawai'i's substantive low- to mid-rise iconic buildings, including the Alexander Young Building and Hotel, Alexander & Baldwin's and Castle & Cooke's distinguished headquarters, and the low-rise exemplary Dillingham Transportation Building. From the late 1960s to the present significant contemporary iconic high-rises have added to Bishop Street's urban quality and ambiance, including First Hawaiian Bank's and Bank of Hawai'i's Headquarters, and during the 1970s and early 1980s AHL's Pacific Trade Center Tower and Grosvenor Center's Twin Towers. During this time, Bishop Street's two most significant open park spaces were created through AHL's planning and design, first at Pacific Trade Center Tower during the early 1970s, then at Grosvenor Center in the late 1970s and early 1980s.

AHL'S CONTRIBUTION TO BISHOP STREET'S SILHOUETTE LEAVES AN ENDURING LEGACY...

PACIFIC TRADE CENTER (PTC) *(currently American Savings Bank Tower)*: Pacific Trade Center Tower is located along Bishop Street *mauka* from the Grosvenor superblock site. In its role as the architect for PTC, Architects Hawaii proposed a phased superblock master plan for a future second high-rise tower and formation of the new urban Tamarind Park concurrent with PTC. Making room for both the development of the second tower and a new urban park came at the cost of demolishing the Alexander Young Building. While the Alexander Young Building was indeed historical, its overall design and quality left much to be desired, especially along its block-long rear façade, which faced the newly created Tamarind Park. Architects Hawaii felt that the overall benefit of the creation of Tamarind Park outweighed the Alexander Young building's demise, hence their master plan proposal. Public meetings and government processes followed together with the governmental entitlement process leading to the approval of Architects Hawaii's proposed master plan.

Construction for Pacific Trade Center (PTC) completed in 1972. PTC's 30 stories, designed to the maximum allowable height of 350 feet, enjoy outstanding views to Bishop Street's bustling activities and the city skyline and beyond. Its structure featured the largest concrete "raft" foundation ever constructed in Hawai'i, and its frame and exterior were of cast-in-place coral aggregate concrete. The façade was hand-hammered, using ribbed formwork, creating a distinctive natural "sandy" Hawaiian look and feel. Open trellises provided shade for pedestrians and visual interest both at grade and the tower's top. Hawaiian petroglyph patterns at the façade's lower level punctuate the building's "sense of place." The indoor-outdoor lobby features vibrant koa wood walls and woven tapestries depicting Polynesian tales designed by Hawai'i artist Herb Kane. The parking structure

was an innovative and highly efficient "double helix" design, devoid of free-standing columns and circulation ramps, the first of its kind in Hawai'i. With PTC's construction completed in 1972, Architects Hawaii moved into its third floor overlooking the newly created Tamarind Park.

The overall superblock master plan came to full fruition in 1984 with the completion of the second envisioned office building, Pauahi Tower, in the superblock named Bishop Square. American Savings Bank became PTC's prime tenant in the early 1990s, and the building's name changed to American Savings Bank Tower.

Honolulu's downtown community embraced Tamarind Park from the onset of its completion. Tamarind Park comprises an acre of generous paving and lawn, large monkeypod trees, water features, and a sculpture by Henry Moore. These components provide an open, attractive, and inviting gathering place for people chatting over coffee, enjoying plate lunch, passing or driving by, or merely lingering along its generous linear seating areas and "watching the world go by" at the bustling intersection of Bishop and King Streets. During the holidays, when its trees are colorfully lit for all in town to enjoy, Tamarind Park's downtown epicenter is especially celebrated. In 1986, Tamarind Park received First Place in the Project of the Year Awards by the City & County of Honolulu.

Architects Hawaii relived the Tamarind Park discussions around demolishing the Alexander Young Building with a second new anticipated high-rise superblock further *makai* on Bishop Street, site of the renowned Dillingham Transportation Building (DTB). The DTB, designed in 1929, richly detailed in the Italian Renaissance/Mediterranean Revival Style, exuded charm and grace inside and out. DTB's superblock site had been bought in the mid-1970s by Gerald Grosvenor, Duke of Westminster, and one of England's richest men. The new owner envisioned demolishing the Dillingham Transportation Building to front his envisioned two new towers on prestigious Bishop Street, giving them a status "high rent" Bishop Street address.

GROSVENOR CENTER *(currently Pacific Guardian Center)*

Shortly after the Grosvenor site purchase, the owners selected Architects Hawaii as architects for the new superblock development, which was named "Grosvenor Center." From the onset, the architects lamented demolishing the Dillingham Transportation Building. Contrary to the Alexander Young Building, they saw the Dillingham Transportation Building's aesthetics and history as high value both to their client's brand and to the community overall. Following their work on Tamarind Park creation and the Hawai'i State Capitol, Architects Hawaii's continued its commitment to enhancing the quality of Honolulu's urban places, spaces, and history.

The architects sought design strategies and approaches to retain the DTB as a viable element in the Grosvenor superblock's overall design. Architects Hawaii's determination resulted in the creation of a new vision achieving its goals for the Grosvenor superblock. Rather than placing the twin towers along Bishop Street, they put them along Alakea Street to the site's rear. This location enabled the creation of a new significant urban park plaza for Honolulu's Downtown community and celebrated the DTB as a free-standing "jewel box" along Bishop Street. The design concept for Grosvenor Center's urban plaza was a serene tropical landscaped oasis. This concept is in contrast with Tamarind Park's openness and high energy connection to the city's pedestrian and vehicular life. Pedestrian access was through newly created arcades in the DTB and opened from Merchant Street with vehicular service and parking located along Alakea Street.

Grosvenor Center's 620,000-square-foot superblock utilizes angular geometry for twin angular high-rise tower buildings and open spaces, playing off and featuring the DTB along Bishop Street. The angular geometry enables highly efficient tower footprints of roughly 12,000-square-feet while maximizing open public space at ground level. The angular geometry enables highly efficient tower footprints of roughly 12,000-square-feet by bringing the tower façade down to the street level and maximizing open public space at ground level. Separate tower entry lobbies at the plaza feature "Living Walls." Pedestrian access to the parking is from the plaza and central between the two towers. The "Live-Work-Play" plaza hosts special gatherings and events for tenants, including Halloween, Christmas, Fourth of July, etc. Throughout the year, its tables and chairs in the lush tree-shaded open space and under DTB arcades are popular with the Downtown community; providing functional usability for dining, meetings, sitting with laptops, reading, etc. Ping pong, chess, and live music abound for tenants and passers-by.

Overall, the architectural towers' design quality is light and geometric. The towers, clad in silver gray glass, become a background for the historic Dillingham Trade Center's "jewel

QUEEN ST
HALEKAUWILA ST

box" presence. The parking structure covered in glass and metal screening, with vertical slit openings, provides outside air circulation. From Bishop Street and beyond, the glass towers blend, adapt with, and become part of the sky's changing colors and forms, featuring views to the DTB at the pedestrian level. Floor-to-ceiling glass provides unique connections for occupants to Honolulu's ocean, mountains, and city skyline.

Grosvenor's Center was purchased in 2001 by Meijiseimei Realty, a subsidiary of Japan's Meiji Company, and renamed Pacific Guardian Center. Under its new ownership, Pacific Guardian Center was awarded LEED-EBOM (Existing Buildings: Operations & Maintenance) Silver Certification in 2012. Through upgrades to the building's air conditioning system and lighting, PGC was able to reduce energy usage to roughly half of what comparable buildings nationwide consume, all while maintaining the same high level of service and comfort for tenants. The LEED-EBOM certification recognizes the policies implemented by the Pacific Guardian Center to reduce water consumption, divert waste from the landfill, use green cleaning products, encourage alternative forms of transportation, and improve the indoor environmental quality of the building.

AHL's contribution to Bishop Street's silhouette leaves an enduring legacy in the form of striking architecture coupled with appreciable open and pleasant urban park spaces. •

PROJECT CREDITS

AMERICAN SAVINGS BANK TOWER

CLIENT
Northwestern Mutual Life Insurance

ARCHITECT
Architects Hawaii Ltd.

CONTRACTOR
Pacific Construction Company

PACIFIC GUARDIAN CENTER

CLIENT
Gerald Grosvenor

ARCHITECT
Architects Hawaii Ltd.

CONTRACTOR
Pacific Construction Company

KAISER PERMANENTE

HONOLULU CLINIC

COMPLETED **1986**

PROJECT CREDITS

CLIENT
Kaiser Permanente Facilities

ARCHITECT
Architects Hawaii Ltd.

CONTRACTOR
McCarthy / Kiewit Joint Venture

Henry Kaiser was a highly successful industrialist who built some of the country's largest projects, including Hoover, Bonneville, and Grand Coulee Dams.

Henry Kaiser founded Kaiser Health Plan in 1958, and constructed Kaiser Hospital in Honolulu shortly after that. Located on a beautiful oceanfront site at the beginning of Waikīkī, the design concept was for a hospital that could convert to a hotel should the need arise to relocate.

That need arose in the early 1980s. When the limited oceanfront site could not accommodate the needed expansion, Kaiser Hospital made the strategic decision to vacate its present facilities and build a new hospital along the H-1 Freeway at Moanalua, the center of gravity for Honolulu's present and future population. Many Kaiser Hospital patients lived or worked near the old location, and Kaiser Permanente also decided to build a new clinic to serve urban Honolulu's present and growing population. Kaiser Permanente retained AHL as architects both for the new Moanalua Hospital and the new Clinic.

Kaiser Permanente Honolulu Clinic opened in 1986. The design concept for the six-story outpatient facility was to accommodate 64 physicians of all specialties plus same-day surgery operating room and complete emergency department. A 440-car parking structure serves patients and staff.

The clean precast concrete exterior featured shading devices for interior comfort and energy conservation. Exposed-concrete interior spaces receive indirect natural light. Glass block and stainless-steel complement the exposed concrete interiors. Large murals and soft furnishings combine with the architecture creating a contemporary, relaxed environment for patients.

In 1987 Architects Hawaii received an AIA Award of Merit from the Hawaii Society of AIA for Kaiser Permanente Honolulu Clinic.

As with many of AHL's large past projects, Kaiser Permanente Clinic continues to offer a clean modernist presence as it serves Honolulu's urban community. •

KE'ELIKOLANI STATE OFFICE BUILDING

Photo: Andrea Brizzi

COMPLETED **1986**

Architects Hawaii was retained in the mid-1980s by the State of Hawai'i to design a new high-rise office building to house several State agencies and departments.

The proposed corner for the State Office Building was part of a city block housing two existing State buildings. The two-story Hale Auhau Tax Office fronting Queen Street was historically and aesthetically notable, while the four-story building along Halekauwila Street was less so. The new high-rise office tower was to be at the corner of Queen and Punchbowl Streets, adjacent to Hale Akau.

Architects Hawaii quickly realized that the new tower plus the two existing buildings would pose several urban design issues. The mix of visually unrelated building forms and façades would be aesthetically problematic and have little relationship with the adjacent US Federal Building complex. Resulting pedestrian open spaces would lack focus. Most importantly, the office tower would be unsympathetic with the Hawai'i State Capitol Master Plan's emphasis on low-rise structures and central green pedestrian outdoor open spaces.

Architects Hawaii addressed these issues by recommending a new planning and design approach for the State Office Building and a fresh vision for the entire city block. The design team proposed a reconfigured program that would envelop the existing four-story building.

The resulting larger office structure maintained the Hawai'i State Capitol District low-rise guidelines and the Civic Center Master Plan. Innovative vertical concrete fins introduced a new overall façade aesthetic to shield interiors from the sun.

The building's quiet modernist textured concrete façade extended the full length of the block, creating a restrained backdrop for the historic State Tax building on Queen Street while simultaneously complementing the adjacent Federal Building complex on Halekauwila Street.

Eliminating the tower opened the site up to generously landscaped pedestrian spaces and a small park at the Queen Street corner. The required floor area "wrapping" left space within the new low-rise office building to create three separate, open courtyards. Fresh air, outdoor circulation, daylight, and visual relief added significant appeal to interior offices. The completion of the State Office Building transformed Mililani Street into a landscaped mall. Overall pedestrian circulation connected with adjacent streets, State and Federal government, 'Iolani Palace, Honolulu Harbor, and beyond.

The State of Hawai'i Department of Accounting and General Services enthusiastically endorsed Architects Hawaii's proposal, and the city block vision came into being. The Ke'elikolani State Office Building received the Hawaii Society's AIA Award of Merit and the City & County of Honolulu's Project of the Year 1988 Honorable Mention Award. •

PROJECT CREDITS

CLIENT
State of Hawai'i, DAGS

ARCHITECT
Architects Hawaii Ltd.

INTERIOR DESIGN
Architects Hawaii Ltd.

CONTRACTOR
Mitsunaga Construction, INC. (Phase I)
Dynamic Industries Corporation (Phase II)

AWARDS

- AIA Honolulu Chapter Award of Merit, 1989
- City & County of Honolulu Project of the Year Award, Honorable Mention, 1988

LILI'UOKALANI GARDENS

COMPLETED **1984**

The 1970s marked a period of increased development in Hawai'i by Japanese investors. Haseko Development, along with several other Japanese developers, established themselves in the islands by building luxury residential towers.

Queen Lili'uokalani's former Waikīkī home, Paoakalani, located at Ala Wai Boulevard and Paoakalani Street, is now the site of Lili'uokalani Gardens. Haseko Development retained Architects Hawaii Ltd. to design small, luxury apartments that would appeal to visitors from Japan and overseas.

Due to the site's historical prominence and proximity to Waikīkī, the design approach required significant planning acumen to incorporate several concepts essential to the site.

The property consumed an entire block, fronting along the Ala Wai Canal, offering stunning views across the canal, through to the mountains, and O'ahu's skyline. The site also provided large landscaping areas at ground level. During the days of the Hawaiian Monarchy, grounds also included a stream, driving the team to adopt "flowing water" as a central design theme. Finally, the integration of art and nature that expressed both Hawaiian and Japanese culture was a crucial concept. The design seamlessly married the cultures of the client and the community to bring Lili'uokalani Gardens to life.

AHL's design concept was for two smaller and more elegant 24-story towers rather than a single massive and monolithic tower. The buildings were juxtaposed to provide the best possible views from the units, comprising a total of 384 studio, one-, and two-bedroom apartments.

AHL's two-tower scheme enabled nearly 70 percent of the site to be dedicated to open space. The natural, landscaped garden was an appealing amenity for residents and was considered "Waikīkī's Largest Private Park." The design includes a stream water feature that meanders through the

garden from one tower to the other, transitioning to a "mosaic stream" of porcelain and glass tiles and murals within lobbies and as the floor of the large outdoor amenity pool.

The radiating vertical fins and striking color palette emphasize the design's verticality and express the fluid sculptural form of the massing. Iconic sculptural elements radiate the exterior 'fin' façade. Since its opening in 1984, Lili'uokalani Gardens stands elegant and distinguished—a "jewel in the crown"—of Waikīkī's Ala Wai Boulevard. •

PROJECT CREDITS

CLIENT
Haseko Development, Inc.

ARCHITECT
Architects Hawaii Ltd.

INTERIOR DESIGN
Architects Hawaii Ltd.

CONTRACTOR
Pacific Construction

ONE WATERFRONT TOWERS

Photo: Andrea Brizzi

COMPLETED **1990**

Kaka'ako's commercial and retail district, located between Honolulu's Downtown to the west and Ala Moana Shopping Center to the east, was historically by low-rise light industrial and related retail buildings.

With its ideal urban Honolulu location, Kaka'ako has long been envisioned as a vibrant, mixed-use urban neighborhood bringing much needed density and activity to the core of Honolulu. One Waterfront Towers was a crucial step in bringing this vision to life and stimulated the transformation of this neighborhood that we see continuing to this day.

One Waterfront Towers was developed by Stark Realty, whose principal, Bruce Stark, believed in strong visual statements for his projects. As a pioneering project for the revitalization of Kaka'ako, One Waterfront Towers is the first project developed under the State's then-new Kaka'ako District Regulations. Through his relationship with design architect Warner Boone on low-rise projects, Stark designed the new twin-tower high-rise development. In turn, Stark chose AHL to join his project team based on AHL's extensive local and overseas high-rise expertise. As both Executive Architect and Architect of Record, AHL took the lead in bringing Boone's signature form concept to reality.

One Waterfront Towers showcases the site's unobstructed ocean, harbor, and downtown views, offering upscale residences in an optimal location, adjacent to Honolulu's central business and financial district. Completed in 1990, the 400-foot twin luxury 45-story high-rises bring uniqueness and vitality to Honolulu's skyline. The project site is situated on South Street just east of

Photo: Adam Taylor

Honolulu's Downtown. The main entrance and amenity areas are located mid-block with towers anchoring the two ends of the site. Individual floors have an average of four apartment units with roughly 40 percent one-bedroom, 50 percent two-bedroom, and 10 percent penthouse units. Amenity areas include a pool, sauna, whirlpool, tennis courts, gym, meeting facilities, and state-of-the-art entry security systems. There are 306 apartment units along with 570 parking stalls.

One Waterfront Towers' distinctive form and façade now add diversity and richness to the Kaka'ako skyline that continues to evolve year after year into the dynamic community always imagined. •

PROJECT CREDITS

CLIENT
Stark Realty

ARCHITECT
Architects Hawaii Ltd.

DESIGN ARCHITECT
Warner Boone

CONTRACTOR
Pacific Construction Co.

WAIKĪKĪ LANDMARK

COMPLETED **1993**

In the early 1990s, AHL won a design competition for a luxury high-rise residential condominium.

Located at Honolulu's prestigious Kalākaua Avenue and Ala Wai Boulevard intersection, the prominent 2.8-acre parcel sat at the east end of Waikīkī near the soon-to-be-built Hawai'i Convention Center, scheduled to open in 1998. Architects Hawaii's winning competition entry focused on the interaction between the building form and heavy pedestrian and vehicular traffic passing through Waikīkī. "Waikīkī Landmark" is fundamentally two 38-story towers connected at the top through a "bridge," forming an iconic "Gateway-to-Waikīkī" urban statement.

Completed in 1993, its 179 luxury residential condominium apartments are bridged at the 33rd floor by ten-foot-deep steel trusses interspersed with mechanical areas. Eighteen penthouses are located on floors 34 – 38, sitting atop towers and the "bridge," providing sweeping views of O'ahu's city form, mountains, and ocean. Open space between the towers is 65 feet. The tightly clustered overall building form enabled 64 percent open space overall on the site. With 11 floors of parking for 570 cars and 39,000-square-feet of commercial space, Waikīkī Landmark's gross area is roughly 675,000-square-feet.

Bringing Architects Hawaii's unique design concept to reality posed significant technical and government approval challenges, including setbacks between buildings and fire protection. Differing soil conditions under each tower required an individual foundation and construction sequencing approach. The anticipated tower settlement and movement differences were accommodated, by providing additional structural stability.

Honolulu's Building Code and Waikīkī's Special Design District Regulations did not anticipate the bridged tower design. Architects Hawaii's close dialogue and collaboration with the City from design through construction enabled ongoing administrative reviews and approvals at each step along the way. Completing the project on schedule and within the owner's budget was a testament to the close teaming by the Waikīkī Landmark owner, Architects Hawaii's design team, and the general contractor.

Waikīkī Landmark's thoughtfully designed open spaces include extensive paving and heavy landscaping along its prominent Kalākaua Avenue, Ala Wai Boulevard, and McCully Street boundaries. Entry porte-cochere, recreation amenity deck, and podium façade elements are also highly landscaped. •

PROJECT CREDITS

CLIENT
Sukamto Holding Corporation

ARCHITECT
Architects Hawaii Ltd.

CONTRACTOR
Charles Pankow Builders

THE QUEEN'S MEDICAL CENTER

COMPLETED **ONGOING**

The Queen's Medical Center is the first hospital in the US established by royalty. In King Kamehameha IV's opening speech to the legislature in 1855, the King proposed creating a hospital for the people of Hawai'i.

The smallpox epidemic of 1853 seriously threatened the continued existence of the Hawaiian race, killing thousands of people in the already dwindling population. In 1859 Queen Emma and King Kamehameha IV raised $13,530, which, together with $6,000 of legislature funding, was used to build Hawai'i's first modern medical facility. The King laid the cornerstone for the two-story 124-bed facility named "House of Kalākaua" in 1860, and Queen Emma herself became its chief volunteer.

The hospital's "Punchbowl" campus grew steadily from the 1950s on. In 1967 its name was changed to The Queen's Medical Center. During that time, preliminary design studies focused on a coordinated Hawai'i medical services growth strategy with The Queen's Medical Center as its epicenter.

From the 1970s to the present, AHL has served as architect and master planner on selected commissions. The relocation of the radiation oncology facility in the late 1970s was the first step in AHL's extensive medical center renovation master plan. Tight site constraints prompted a below-grade building design solution with an at grade landscaped roof for patients and staff relaxation.

Immediately adjacent to the Radiation Oncology building is AHL's five-story exposed-aggregate concrete Cancer Center of Hawaii, completed in 1979. In the 2000s, the Cancer Center moved into AHL's newly expanded

John A. Burns School of Medicine in Kaka'ako. The 1979 Cancer Center building became part of The Queen's Medical Center and was named "Lauhala Building."

Construction of AHL's 425,000-square-foot Queen Emma Tower began in the late 1980s. Facilities provided in the complex include new care units for critically ill or injured patients and a range of new or replacement medical state-of-the-art systems. Among the updated systems were radiographic services, nuclear medicine and ultrasound, advanced computerization, material management, administration, and foodservice. The design focus was on patient quality of experience, including calming interiors and a lush green garden viewed from most patient rooms.

More than doubling emergency space, the new trauma center provides ambulance docking, psychiatric ward, decontamination, emergency surgery, examination and consultation, as well as waiting and children's play areas.

The ER's long two-story form wraps around the existing mixture of functional building forms created over time in the Medical Center's growth and development process. Together with extensive landscaping and reconsideration of drop-off and pick-up, the new ER façade projects a reinvigorated "Hawaiian Sense of Place" image to Honolulu's community overall. Responding to the Historic District contextual design guidelines, the ER's pitched roof forms and deep arcades provide a sense of welcome and hospitality. All in all, the ER expresses The Queen's Medical Center's legacy mission, vision, and brand.

AHL's recently completed five-story Pauahi Tower façade replacement extends this "Hawaiian Sense of Place" vernacular, providing related background to the ER and Medical Center's overall "front door" image and entrance experience.

As of the publishing of this book, AHL continues to support The Queen's Medical Center's dynamic response to today's accelerated change in its facilities at The Queen's Medical Center and throughout the State of Hawai'i. •

PROJECT CREDITS

CLIENT

The Queen's Health Systems

ARCHITECT

Architects Hawaii Ltd. ; AHL

UNIVERSITY OF HAWAI'I

HAWAI'I HALL RENOVATION

COMPLETED **2002**

Constructed in 1912 as the first permanent building erected on campus, the University of Hawai'i's Hawai'i Hall brilliantly portrays Architect Hawaii's experience in adaptively reusing historical structures.

The design team took great care in retaining this Classical Revival building's character, defining details, including its Doric columns, when renovating this significant structure that anchors the campus's historic quadrangle.

Hawai'i Hall provides 37,000-square-feet of administrative spaces for the College of Arts and Sciences, Academic Affairs, and Student Academic Services. Interior design elements maintain a traditional Hawaiian aesthetic while integrating modern modular workstations.

Distinguished by its grand two-story Doric columns, a cornice with dentils, and a pedimented parapet, this three-story Neo-Classical building is also an early example of reinforced concrete construction in the islands.

Due to structural issues, the interior required complete demolition, while retaining the second-floor stair rail and wood trim for reuse. The design team meticulously reproduced the doors and transoms to match existing conditions and meet present-day building code standards. The arch brackets in the corridors were salvaged and reused in the same manner as the original design.

The 37,000-square-feet of interior space includes three stories of office space for the Colleges of Arts and Sciences; Humanities; Social Sciences; Natural Sciences; and Language, Linguistics, and Literature. Services included complete interior design and furnishings for new modular workstations.

Architects Hawaii's renovation of Hawai'i Hall received design awards and recognition from several esteemed organizations including the American Public Works Association's "Project of the Year Award" for design excellence.•

PROJECT CREDITS

CLIENT

University of Hawai'i Mānoa

ARCHITECT

Architects Hawaii Ltd.

AWARDS

- American Public Works Association Historical Restoration / Preservation Project of the Year, 2003
- AIA Honolulu Award of Merit, 2003
- General Contractors Association Build Hawaii Merit Award, 2004
- NAIOP Kukulu Hale Award, Historical Project of the Year, 2004

MARRIOTT'S KO OLINA BEACH CLUB

COMPLETED **2003–2011**

In the 2000s, Marriott Vacation Club International announced plans to build the brand's largest location, a flagship timeshare development on the 28-acre oceanfront site fronting on a 3.5-acre lagoon-front beach.

Ko Olina is a master-planned community of 642 acres, including a golf course and a marina. Marriott's Ko Olina Beach Club would become the initial new timeshare development in Hawai'i and the first new significant development at Ko Olina Resort in nine years. This development kickstarted an unprecedented era of resort construction on O'ahu's west side and has grown into a premier destination for tourists and locals alike.

Marriott developed the design program around anticipated timeshare sales over extended periods. Sales requirements were significant, with 750 two- and three-bedroom units requiring construction to be completed over seven phases.

Upon selection, AHL implemented a concept addressing and resolving the existing site and setback, envisioning a new design with four v-shaped towers rather with each leg of the "V" becoming a separate phase. Minimizing the number of towers greatly enhanced the open spaces between them and resultant views within the grounds and beyond. Tower orientations took maximum advantage of the spectacular views of the Wai'anae coastline and open ocean. The angular shapes and siting produced ever-changing building massing as one moves within the site, throughout Ko Olina, and from neighboring areas near and far. Tower forms, articulated through

Photo: Hai Lum

stepping façade configurations, provide individual character to each tower. Natural stone and rusticated plaster blend with extensive landscaping, forming a rugged and natural feel to indoor-outdoor building-site relationships. Resulting view corridors, which additionally enhanced the guest experience, were of importance to the community.

The conversion to four larger towers also proved to be highly efficient by minimizing the number of exit stairs and elevators. With the towers completed on the exterior, the future phase of each building leg was an unfinished shell with interior drywall and other materials stored inside. As sales generated completion for each "V" leg, contractors finished interior spaces with minimal effects on the Beach Club's overall ambiance and guest experience.

The first-phase tower contained the main lobby and guest arrival facilities, establishing the overall character and quality of the development at full buildout. Enhanced overall arrival experience was created by raising the entry drive and lobby over 15 feet, providing commanding views over the beach lagoon out to the open ocean. Reception facilities featured registration, lobby, concierge, activities, and tour services. Sales facilities housed a welcome center and sales center. Vacation owner amenities included a kid's club, video arcade, billiards room, marketplace, equipment rentals, activities areas, swimming pools, spa, pool bar and grill, and restaurant and deli spaces. The remaining towers primarily provide guestroom units and are situated on grade.

From its time of conception to the present, Marriott's Ko Olina Beach Club has successfully created the feel of a luxury vacation resort in a high-rise timeshare development, infusing airy, island living throughout public areas, units, and landscape. •

PROJECT CREDITS

CLIENT
Marriott Vacations Worldwide

ARCHITECT
Architects Hawaii Ltd.

INTERIOR DESIGN
Pamela Temples Interiors

CONTRACTOR
Nordic PCL,
Dick Pacific Construction

KĀHALA NUI

Photo: Doug Pebbles

COMPLETED **2005**

Built to support Hawai'i's growing senior community, Kāhala Nui's living environments range from 270 privately owned one-, two-, and three-bedroom residences to continuous care in later stages of life, including skilled nursing and memory support.

Located in Honolulu's Wai'alae-Kāhala neighborhood, Kāhala Nui has direct access to public transportation and Kahala Mall and is one of Honolulu's most successful retirement developments. As with many continuing care residential communities, Kāhala Nui was conceived integrally with an institution, Star of the Sea Parish School. The school contributed land in exchange for a new Early Learning Center, provided to the school at no cost. Architects Hawaii's site design utilized land fronting on Malia Street for five- and six-story buildings with excellent views of East Honolulu and across the school's soccer field to the ocean. The soccer field was excavated, and a three-level, 406-car underground parking structure was constructed. The grassed soccer field was then restored over the underground parking, and covered walkways, courtyards, tropical gardens, and fishponds were provided.

Photo: David Franzen

Photo: Douglas Pebbles

Photo: Douglas Pebbles

A variety of luxurious amenities are provided for residents, including indoor and outdoor dining, auditorium, library, wine collection room, hair salon, club room, specialized senior fitness center, pool, and crafts room. Amenity activities and programs include education, social, and culinary services.

Design and planning focused on separation between independent living and facilities in support of nursing and end of life. Kāhala Nui's independent living porte-cochere and main lobby prominently face Malia Street, while the Skilled Nursing Unit has an intentionally discreet entrance at the edge of the site. The separation concept extended throughout the facility and drove the design of dining rooms, lounges, and patient bedrooms.

Achieving residential character and scale was a significant factor in AHL's design process. Extensive landscaping within and along site edges included onsite relocation of mature existing trees that could not be kept in place. The total building area of over 500,000-square-feet was broken up into six structures, maintaining and reinforcing Wai'alae Nui's modest low-rise neighborhood character and scale, which developed over the past 50 years. Since its completion in 2005, Kāhala Nui has become a family and friends gathering place and a truly integral part of the Wai'alae-Kāhala Community. •

PROJECT CREDITS

CLIENT
Greystone Development Company, LLC

ARCHITECT
Architects Hawaii Ltd.

CONTRACTOR
Nordic PCL

HONOLULU ZOO

DISCOVERY CENTER COMPLEX

Photo: Andrea Brizzi

COMPLETED **2006**

In 1876 King Kalākaua made royal lands near the slopes of Diamond Head available for the establishment of a grand public park for the people of his kingdom. A year later, after beautification of the marshes, ponds, and lagoons, Queen Kapi'olani Park opened.

King Kalākaua continued using the park for his collection of exotic birds and horses, and the assortment grew over time. In 1896 the City & County of Honolulu assumed control over Kapi'olani Park. Following Ben Hollinger's appointment as Administrator of Parks & Recreation 18 years later, the park's animal population continued to grow, with additions including a monkey, a sun bear, and several lion cubs. In 1916 a steamship journeying from Australia to Canada dropped off an African Elephant named Daisy, an occasion for celebration and officially forming the Honolulu Zoo. By the end of the 1940s, the collection included a Bactrian camel, sea lions, and several species of birds and monkeys. Over ensuing years of planning and improvements, today's 42-acre Honolulu Zoo has provided education and delight for people of all ages.

Architect Hawaii's was selected as architect in 2006 by the City & County of Honolulu to design the new *Keiki* (Children's) Zoo and teamed with the Seattle-based zoo consultant Portico Group. As a central component in the Discovery Center Complex, the Keiki Zoo's mission was to communicate insight and connection to the tropical world's natural environment.

The Keiki Zoo provides an exciting children's learning environment in safe surroundings. A country feeling flows throughout the site with animals including geese, guinea pigs, koi, lizards, turtles, pigs, goats, a cow, a llama, and a horse. Interactive exhibits include tunnels and water wheels. The collaborative design-assist project delivery process brought experiential design ideas to reality within scope, budget, and schedule.

The discovery center design embraces Hawai'i's rural and agrarian history. Designed around a central pond, structures are inspired by traditional zoo and farm building forms with simple and straightforward details and connections. Playful and interactive design elements engage the children and parents in learning about the animals in the center and at the zoo.

Since its opening in 2007, Honolulu Zoo Discovery Center's Keiki Zoo has delighted countless visitors of all ages and locals. That year AHL received an Award of Merit from AIA Honolulu for the Discovery Center – Keiki Zoo. •

PROJECT CREDITS

CLIENT
City & County of Honolulu

ARCHITECT
Architects Hawaii Ltd.

ZOO CONSULTANT
The Portico Group

Photo: Andrea Brizzi

MOANA PACIFIC

COMPLETED

2007

Photos: Andrea Brizzi

LOCATED IN THE KAKA‘AKO SPECIAL DESIGN DISTRICT, MOANA PACIFIC’S PROMINENT FORMS AND CLEAN EXTERIOR SKIN COMPLEMENT HAWAI‘I’S SKY AND THE OCEAN.

At a time when only luxury, high-end residences were being built, the developer wanted to respond to market conditions and provide a more affordable option for local residents.

Moana Pacific offers an amenity-filled lifestyle environment that reduced commute times and provides the residents with an increased quality of life.

Envisioned as a high-density urban Honolulu thoroughfare, Kapi'olani Boulevard's development was mostly transitional while nearby Waikīkī and Downtown growth was robust.

Completed in 2007, Moana Pacific's iconic twin 46-story elliptical towers marked a considerable design step forward in the City's transition from post-modernism to minimalism. Located in the Kaka'ako Special Design District, Moana Pacific's prominent forms and clean exterior skin complement Hawai'i's sky and the ocean. The Pensacola Street entrance court of the complex creates a residential feeling of quiet calm from neighboring Kapi'olani Boulevard's dense retail environment. Collaborative development with the adjoining Inspiration Furniture site fronting busy Kapi'olani Boulevard created a sculptural mixed-use superblock featuring urban design quality. Each tower includes a total of 354 condominium units ranging from one to three bedrooms plus penthouse units up to 5,000-square-feet each. The twin towers sit atop a six-story parking and lobby podium. Common amenities at the sixth podium level include theaters, party and game rooms, a fitness center, tennis courts, jogging tracks, a putting green, and driving range.

Despite its soaring size, Moana Pacific's mirrored towers stand timelessly, blending in with the ever-changing skies. The elliptical form complements the profiles of the neighboring residential and light-industrial properties. As one of the earliest projects in the long-planned revitalization of Kaka'ako, Moana Pacific is a vibrant and contemporary addition that helps to increase the value of business and properties in the area. •

PROJECT CREDITS

CLIENT
KC Rainbow Development Co. LLC

ARCHITECT
Architects Hawaii Ltd.

CONTRACTOR
Hawaiian Dredging Construction Company

PACIFIC AVIATION MUSEUM

Photo: Andrea Brizzi

COMPLETED **2007**

The Japanese attack on Pearl Harbor on December 7, 1941, included significant damage to four Air Force Hangars on Ford Island.

In 1999, the three surviving hangars, Hangar 37, Hangar 79, and Hangar 54, came under the jurisdiction of a Hawai'i-based non-profit with the mission of telling the story of the US Military Aviation in the Pacific.

The design concept for the Pearl Harbor Aviation Museum encompassed both the historic hangar buildings and the exhibits within. While the ultimate buildout envisioned all three hangars, Hangar 37, at approximately 28,000-square-feet, was chosen for the first phase buildout. Architects Hawaii was selected as architect for the museum portion and commenced work on Hangar 37, which opened on December 7, 2007, the 65th anniversary of the attack on Pearl Harbor.

The design methodology focused on balancing the preservation of historical aspects with the creation of a modern, functional museum. The Hawai'i State Historic Preservation Division (SHPD) required the building exteriors remain mostly unchanged, including bullet holes and other aspects related to the attack. The outside of Hangar 37 lacked an appropriate entry statement and the historic façade could not be modified. Architects Hawaii proposed a fabric structure awning with a checkered pattern echoing external aviation graphics and SHPD approved the design. Hangar 37's high-ceiling interior space and exposed steel structures features exhibits and aircraft. Additional museum functional spaces included an entry lobby, theater, museum shop, restaurant, and administration.

Photo: Andrea Brizzi

The entry floor became a unique design feature that proved highly successful. Reprocessed aerial photos of Pearl Harbor and nearby surroundings into floor tiles enabled visitors to "fly over" as they entered and departed the museum. Circa the 1980s, the photos allow families to recognize their home, parks, school, and other common areas, to reduce the visual impact of the attack in deference to the museum's many yearly visitors from Japan.

Following an increase in visitation over the first few years after opening, the museum began additionally utilizing Hangar 79. Architects Hawaii worked with the Pacific Aviation Museum on the hangars' interim maintenance and improvements, enabling it for museum use and special events. Over 87,000-square-feet in area, Hangar 79's immense clear-span steel truss structure allowed the museum to continue adding to its aircraft collection, which was nearly 40 in 2020. Planes include an A6M2-21 Japanese Zero, a Boeing Stearman Model 75 flown by President George H. W. Bush, and the remains of a B-17 bomber called "Swamp Ghost" that crashed in a marsh after being attacked by nine Japanese fighters in 1942. Also housed in Hangar 79, the Museum's Restoration Shop continues bringing new collection aircraft up to exhibit status.

Ultimately, all three hangars will be joined together, forming Pearl Harbor Aviation Museum's fully operational, restored, repurposed, and historically relevant complex. •

PROJECT CREDITS

CLIENT
Pacific Aviation Museum

ARCHITECT
Architects Hawaii Ltd.

CONTRACTOR
Kiewit Building Group

Photo: Andrea Brizzi

UNIVERSITY OF HAWAI'I

JOHN A. BURNS SCHOOL OF MEDICINE

COMPLETED

2008

Photo: Andrea Brizzi

Following WWII, a Honolulu police officer named John A. Burns founded a political movement through garnering the support of the impoverished sugar plantation workers, which restored strength to the divided Democratic Party of Hawai'i. That police officer would eventually serve as Hawai'i's second Governor from 1962 to 1974.

Burns also gained support from Japanese American veterans of the 100th Infantry Battalion and 442nd Infantry Regiments returning home, encouraging them to become educated under the GI Bill and run for public office. Daniel K. Inouye was one of the first veterans he recruited and a prominent member of the movement. In 1962 Inouye was elected to the United States Senate and remained in office for 50 years until his passing in 2012. During those years, he chaired various Senate Committees, including Intelligence, Commerce, Indian Affairs, and Appropriations.

As designers for the John A. Burns School of Medicine (JABSOM), Architects Hawaii's role included master planning and architectural and interior design. JABSOM's delivery time frame was politically sensitive. The JABSOM project was initiated by the State's response to 9/11's devastating effect on Hawai'i's economy, and developed under a unique program of the University of Hawai'i Research Corporation. JABSOM's mission and goal was to significantly increase biomedical research and related start-ups activity to kindle a formidable and innovative bioscience industry in Hawai'i.

JABSOM is located entirely separate from the University of Hawai'i's Mānoa Campus. The location encourages interaction and collaboration with Downtown Honolulu's prominent corporations, banks, and medical centers.

Photo: Andrea Brizzi

THE $150-MILLION FACILITY HOUSES A BIOMEDICAL RESEARCH AND EDUCATION CENTER THAT ATTRACTS SIGNIFICANT FEDERAL FUNDING AND PRIVATE SECTOR INVESTMENT IN BIOTECH AND CANCER RESEARCH AND DEVELOPMENT.

The UH School of Medicine sits on a 9.9-acre site between Kaka'ako Park and the former Gold Bond Building, in Honolulu's Kaka'ako Special Design District. There are four buildings on the campus, including an Education/Administration Building, a Biomedical Research Building, a Staff Fitness and Childcare Center facility, and a Central Utilities Plant. The design of the central landscaped courtyard on the campus provides a gathering space at the foot of the Education/Administration Building. The center of the courtyard houses the School of Medicine Dean's office, metaphorically acting as the heart of the campus and the program. From that starting point, all pathways and landscape radiate outward, bringing life and activity to a once neglected area of Honolulu.

JABSOM's delivery time frame was logistically remarkable. Regarded as an economic engine for the State, the project's mission was to jump-start the economy ASAP through the creation of quality jobs, biomedical research activity, and national recognition as the stimulus for an emerging biotechnical industry in Hawai'i.

Photo: Andrea Brizzi

JABSOM's accelerated design and delivery schedule rapidly advanced through site determination and start-up in August 2001, groundbreaking in October 2002, and completion and opening in September 2005. The $150-million facility houses a biomedical research and education center that attracts significant federal funding and private sector investment in biotech and cancer research and development. Faculty in the Department of Cell and Molecular Biology have ongoing research programs in areas including genetics, cell biology, biochemistry, and neurophysiology.

JABSOM was designed and built in three closely overlapping phases: Medical Education Building, Biomedical Sciences Building, and Ancillary/Central Plant/Site. These staggered phases allowed construction to begin at one end of the site, while existing tenants on the other portions of the site completed their leases. Staggered phasing enabled timely occupancy by the University following the initial phase, while construction of the more complex research facility concluded. To further accelerate construction, design and construction documents and permitting packages were separated for demolition and site, foundation, underground utilities, and building. The result was 12 design/pricing/permit/contract packages comprising three closely overlapping phases.

Design inspiration for JABSOM emanated from Architects Hawaii's commitment to an engaging and collaborative process. Together with historic partners and cultural practioners, AHL also engaged with JABSOM research scientists to better understand their philosophy, mission, and goals. As a result, JABSOM's aesthetic blends a sense of Hawaiian culture and community with the philosophy of present and future science, expressed literally and abstractly, through ancient and contemporary ideas, themes, and imagery.

The building was constructed using heavy precast concrete panels, which double as the structural system as well as the architectural wall finish. The façade is intricately detailed with reliefs featuring Hawaiian *kapa* (Hawaiian bark cloth)-inspired motifs in a band wrapping the perimeter of the exterior. The theme merges the scientific codes of DNA strands with ancient Hawaiian patterns of wind, rain, water, and cane. Borrowing from Hawaiian legend about the gods *Kāne* and *Lono*, the building's design includes soaring spaces, tall vertical elements, and abundant use of natural sunlight.

Photo: Andrea Brizzi

Heavy precast concrete tees are structurally tied to the exterior walls, creating a frame that meets the exacting vibration requirements of the research facility. Woven through the center lobbies of each of the buildings are four-story-high glazed curtain walls. This design compliments the natural acid-etched concrete finish with the smooth and contemporary look of glass and steel, giving the buildings "a high-tech high-touch feel." As a campus, the structures balance the technologically advanced needs of the science programs with the aesthetic desire to provide the community with a project that reflects a Hawaiian sense of place.

JABSOM's innovative cold seawater well system for central cooling was initiated by the University of Hawai'i Board of Regents together with the Board of Water Supply. Using cold seawater pumped from deep wells to help run JABSOM's air-conditioning system significantly reduced the University's usage of electricity and resultant operating costs. It also reduced the use of O'ahu's potable water and demonstrated and promoted the use of deep-well seawater cooling systems for other projects. JABSOM's deep seawater cooling system was one of many energy-saving features that enabled the project to achieve LEED certification, one of Hawai'i's earliest major projects to do so.

Included as part of the requirements by the University of Hawai'i, the project received USGBC LEED Certification and has implemented many green building aspects into its design. By affirming healthcare's fundamental mission of "first, do no harm," the University of Hawai'i John A. Burns School of Medicine recognizes the profound impact of the built environment on the health of occupants, local communities, and global ecology. By attaining LEED Certification for the facility, the school encourages design strategies that enhance the learning environment for students, healthy and productive work environments for staff, and responsible ecological stewardship.

In addition to revitalizing the UH Medical School program, the $150 million JABSOM complex functions as an economic engine for the State that creates quality jobs, increases biomedical research activity, and serves as a stimulus for a robust bio-technical industry in Hawai'i. •

PROJECT CREDITS

CLIENT
University of Hawai'i

ARCHITECT
Architects Hawaii Ltd.

INTERIOR DESIGN
Architects Hawaii Ltd.

CONTRACTOR
Hawaiian Dredging Construction Company

DESIGN PRINCIPLES

- Design a premier, sustainable educational facility for Hawai'i's future medical professionals
- Incorporate Hawaiian motifs, kapa patterns, and etchings of Hawaiian healing plants
- Traditional massing and forms integrated with modern materials and methods

SPARK M. MATSUNAGA

VETERANS AFFAIRS MEDICAL CENTER

Photo: Andrea Brizzi

COMPLETED **2008**

The Spark Matsunaga VA Medical Center opened in 2000 following a 30-year process, which began in the late 1970s when US Senator Spark Matsunaga originally proposed the idea to Congress.

Senator Matsunaga's perseverance carried through to 1987 when he received a promise from the Department of Veterans Affairs for construction of the medical center in Hawai'i.

Upon his passing in 1990, President George H. W. Bush signed into law measures naming the facility after Matsunaga. With backing from Senators Inouye and Akaka, continued support pursuing the process made the medical center a reality.

In the early 1990s, the Department of Veterans Affairs (VA) announced plans to proceed with a veteran's facility at the historic Tripler Army Medical Center. Tripler's humble origins began with several wooden structures, constructed in 1907, which were eventually replaced by more extensive buildings, culminating in its present facility, built during World War II that averages roughly 2,000 patients per day.

Tripler's historic, iconic, and imposing "military deco" structure sits on the Moanalua ridge's prominent hillside with O'ahu's dramatic mountains framing its backdrop. Tripler's signature coral pink color was a personal choice of General Robert C. Richardson Jr., the Military Governor of the Territory of Hawai'i during World War II, who borrowed the color and other design elements from Waikīkī's Royal Hawaiian Hotel. Long a landmark for Hawai'i's residents and visitors alike, the VA set an overall visual goal of siting the new buildings behind Tripler such that any new structures would be hidden from view until one drives past and uphill of the Army Medical Center.

Photos: Andrea Brizzi

Architects Hawaii was appointed as the architect and began design in 1993. Architects Hawaii's principal planning goal was to provide exterior circulation and building functionality while meeting the visual goals to site individual building elements on the hilly terrain.

The full facility complex consisted of four major program elements:

1. Renovation and repurposing of Tripler's four-story E Wing hospital ward into VA Regional Offices
2. Sixty-bed Regional Center for Aging
3. 105-bed Medical Center
4. 600-car-capacity parking structure

An additional challenge was how to phase the design to align with funding and the overall project schedule that targeted a facility complex in operation toward the end of the 1990s. The 40,000-square-foot Regional Center for Aging consists of a 45-bed nursing home care unit, a 15-bed memory care unit, adult daycare facilities, and a comprehensive physical therapy department. The 92,000-square-foot medical center includes a dental clinic and lab, pharmacy, radiology center, laboratory, eye and prosthetics, women's health, and mental health facilities. Implementation was phased in separate packages in sync with appropriations, move-in, and overall project scheduling.

Architects Hawaii's comprehensive design approach focused on incorporating contemporary design elements within Tripler's distinct historic vernacular. Calming interior palettes, clear wayfinding, and creating a "non-institutional" healing environment were principal priorities. The Regional Center for Aging provides a personal and intimate patient experience. From the patient arrival to the treatment spaces, the Medical Center projects the government's unwavering commitment to our veterans.

The Spark Matsunaga VA Medical Center's Dedication Ceremony was on June 1, 2000, and they commenced serving 150,000 veterans in Hawai'i and the Pacific. •

PROJECT CREDITS

CLIENT

Department of Veterans Affairs at Tripler Army Medical Center

ARCHITECT

Architects Hawaii Ltd.

THE MOANA SURFRIDER, A WESTIN RESORT

COMPLETED RENOVATION **2007**

Honolulu landowner Walter Chamberlain Peacock started the Moana Hotel Company in 1896, with a plan to establish a fine resort in Honolulu's previously neglected Waikīkī.

Peacock retained architect Oliver G. Traphagen to draw plans for the 75 room Moana Hotel and the Lucas Brothers, who also built 'Iolani Palace, completed construction in 1901. The *Moana* (open sea or ocean) marked the beginning of tourism in Waikīkī, becoming the first hotel amidst Waikīkī's bungalows and beach houses. Peacock's business plan proved untenable, and he sold the hotel to prominent Honolulu businessman Alexander Young. Young then operated it through the early Great Depression and sold it to Matson Navigation in 1932.

Matson's ownership added two floors along with Italian Renaissance-styled wings flanking the hotel, creating the familiar "H" shape seen today. In 1952 Matson built a new taller hotel adjacent to the Moana on the southeast "Diamond Head" side, named the Surfrider Hotel.

The Moana's architecture was influenced by a hybrid of American and European styles fashionable in the early 1900s with Traphagen saying the hotel was "designed for Honolulu alone" and features Ionic columns and intricate woodwork and plaster detailing throughout. Design features included the iconic porte-cochere on Kalākaua Ave and wide lanais on the ocean side. The original hotel program included amenities like a billiard room, saloon, central parlor, reception area, and library; and the first electric powered elevator in the islands, which is still in use today. The generously sized hallways were designed to accommodate the steamer trucks that brought the guests on their trans-pacific voyage. Guest rooms featured bathrooms and telephones, both unusual at the time, plus high ceilings and cross-ventilation windows.

Photos: Andrea Brizzi

EXIT

The Moana Surfrider's oceanfront lanai features an extraordinary Indian Banyan Tree, which was planted in 1904 and maintains a place on Hawai'i's Rare and Exceptional Tree List. From 1935 to 1975, the Moana's oceanfront plaza hosted the Hawai'i Calls live radio broadcast, which was famous throughout the US.

Matson sold the Moana and Surfrider to Japanese industrialist Kenji Osano's Kyo-Ya Company in 1963. Modifications under Kyo-Ya included the historic restoration of the 1901 structure and incorporation of the Surfrider hotel into a single beachfront resort, "Sheraton Moana Surfrider." The Moana Surfrider's restoration efforts received recognition through acceptance of the President's Award for Historic Preservation in 1992.

During 2006 Kyo-Ya appointed Architects Hawaii to realize their vision of upgrading and repositioning the Moana Surfrider from a Sheraton to the Westin brand.

The crux of Architects Hawaii's design assignment was to successfully incorporate Westin's contemporary brand standards while maintaining the Moana's historical integrity and significance. In addition to aesthetic issues, a notable design challenge was that Westin's brand standards required room sizes and features that could not be accommodated in the Moana's smaller sized and irregularly shaped guestrooms.

The design vision focused on delivering the unique Westin brand experience wrapped in the Moana's historic setting. The design team immersed themselves in the Westin's guest experience and all the brand details from service and style to colors and furnishings. This rigorous effort provided the foundation for the project and helped create the Moana's Beachhouse, and Veranda dining venues. The design provided a distinct focus on the Moana's Beachhouse, Veranda, and other uniquely experiential dining venues.

Architects Hawaii achieved its design goals in restoring the timeless elegance that Waikīkī's first hotel has always epitomized, and in so doing, re-established its time-honored position as the "First Lady of Waikīkī." •

PROJECT CREDITS

CLIENT
Kyo-ya Hotels & Resorts, LP

ARCHITECT
Architects Hawaii Ltd.

INTERIOR DESIGN
Looney & Associates

CONTRACTOR
Allied Builders Systems

THE SHOPS

AT WAILEA, MAUNA LANI, KUKUI'ULA

COMPLETED **2009**

Hawai'i's first neighbor island resorts housed three main elements: a hotel, golf course, and residential condominiums. Retail was mostly of a convenience nature, with visitors' main shopping experiences in nearby towns. As neighbor island resorts grew, properties sprawled across hotels and condominiums, justifying enhanced retail spaces.

In effect, the resort became a village with a unique brand. The nearby town then defined its brand differently from the property through a more deep-rooted history and culture with a broader range of offerings. As a result, the overall more significant resort and nearby village worked to complement each other and developed a jointly defined brand.

These trends remained until the late 1990s at the Grand Wailea Resort on Maui, then Hawai'i's fastest developing neighbor island, shortly after that spreading to the Mauna Lani Resort on the Big Island; and then to the Kukui'ula Resort on Kaua'i. Architects Hawaii's selection as architects for Maui's The Shops at Wailea then led to the commissioning for The Shops at Mauna Lani, and later for The Shops at Kukui'ula.

Design for each of Architects Hawaii's "Shops" projects was particular to each property's size, history, culture, and guest experience. Wailea was well-established with multiple hotels, timeshares, and condominiums. Mauna Lani was smaller with an exceptional luxury hotel and residence. Kukui'ula was developing, also luxury, and smaller by nature and intent.

Photo:Bad Moon Saloon / Max Kim

THE SHOPS AT WAILEA

Designed in 1997, The Shops at Wailea is a 150,000-square-foot retail shopping center featuring fine dining and national luxury retailers, including Louis Vuitton, Tiffany's, St. John, Celine, and Tommy Bahama. It maintains an atmosphere and finish level consistent with the quality of the adjacent Grand Wailea Maui and the nearby Four Seasons Resort at Wailea. The property's two-level configuration, sited on a gently inclined 16-acre site, relates to the slope, offering ground floor access for both levels, a critical factor in retail leasing. Three outdoor retail courts are formed by buildings gently stepping down the slope. Luxury retail inhabits the upper court, main street retail on the larger center court, and branded restaurants and shops on the lower, ocean-oriented court. The architectural style is Hawaiian Territorial, with studied variation of stepping building shapes, façades, and roof configurations for the sloping site.

THE SHOPS AT MAUNA LANI

Designed in the early 2000s, the Big Island's Shops at Mauna Lani Resort is a 92,000-square-foot complex offering luxury shopping and dining experiences in seven separate buildings surrounding a pedestrian mall. The Shops addresses demand throughout the surrounding corridor, which attracts highly affluent visitors. Design features include a territorial, low-scale "village" architecture and a "center stage" court for events and entertainment.

THE SHOPS AT KUKUI'ULA

Designed in 2004, Kukui'ula Resort is rooted in the "Garden Isle's" architectural and rural cultural history. Kukui'ula Resort reflects Kaua'i's strong connection with its *paniolo* (cowboy) and sugar plantation past with a rural village concept set in natural, green farm surroundings.

The Shops at Kukui'ula, envisioned to provide a second gathering place at Kukui'ula, offer 91,000-square-feet of retail space. Architects Hawaii's design approach for The Shops was to create a retail village in its historical sense. Nine different retail buildings were sited, creating a variety of casual spaces for intimate wandering to larger gatherings and entertainment venues. Architects Hawaii's designs reflected Kaua'i's quaint old ranch houses in reds, greens, and browns; honoring Kaua'i's "mom-and-pop"-shop-style cottages' simple design materials, exposed wood trim, open-air lanais, and organic colors.

The visitor industry continued to develop and grow, including urban travel destinations, and the need for retail was increasingly recognized. As resort retail expanded, the shopping experience became a critically important "leg of the hospitality table" in the overall property's brand and bottom line.

PROJECT CREDITS

WAILEA

CLIENT
Wailea Retail Associates

ARCHITECT
Architects Hawaii Ltd.

DESIGN ARCHITECT
D'Agostino Izzo Quirk Architects

CONTRACTOR
Hawaiian Dredging Construction Company

MAUNA LANI

CLIENT
Maryl Group, Inc.

ARCHITECT
Architects Hawaii Ltd.

CONTRACTOR
Ledcor US Pacific

KUKUI'ULA

CLIENT
DMB Associates / A&B Properties

ARCHITECT
Architects Hawaii Ltd.

DESIGN ARCHITECT
Callison Architecture

CONTRACTOR
Unlimited Construction Services, Inc.

2012–PRESENT

A VISION FOR THE FUTURE

Hawai'i is responding. Both the firm and the state experienced tremendous growth in the previous decades. Now, in the coming years, we all must address the environmental challenges from that growth. AHL decided that with the changing demands of the future and the limitations of the firm's current workspace, it was time for a new start in a new space that reflected the diversity, transparency, and progressive spirit of the firm.

In 2012, the firm and its staff, now over 90, moved down Bishop Street to the top floor of the AHL-designed Pacific Guardian Center. Walls and offices disappeared to allow the stunning *mauka* and *makai* views to be visible to everyone. An open, modern, sustainable, and digitally enhanced workspace emerged, serving as a model for countless other office spaces in town.

True to our founder's vision, AHL's current projects display a vast array of diversity. Recent projects include a multi-campus master plan for The Queen's Health Systems, O'ahu's first new shopping center in decades, three new judicial complexes, Disney's first themed resort, two performing arts centers, and a new jail. The firm also led a major one percent project to design and renovate an historic structure to create the state's first healing transition center for sexually exploited young women.

Always innovating, a new century demanded a new approach to the firm's philosophy toward the built environment. This century is asking more of us. It's asking for leadership and vision to create a more sustainable community that is responsive to an ever-changing dynamic. AHL, and Hawai'i, are responding to the challenge.

RONALD T.Y. MOON JUDICIARY COMPLEX

Photo: Bad Moon Salon / Max Kim

COMPLETED **2010**

The Ronald T.Y. Moon Judiciary complex responds to the rising demand for judicial services in rapidly growing West O'ahu.

The Complex provides a new courthouse for the First Circuit Family Court and Juvenile Detention Facility with 13 new courtrooms, holding cells, judges' chambers, public service areas, and administrative spaces. A three-part circulation system allows judges, staff, detainees, and the public to move separately with privacy and security. The courthouse utilized the latest in digital recording technology and security system software to make the proceeding more accurate, safe, and secure.

The complex integrates the court and juvenile detention facilities, representing an evolution to a more humane, community-based, and secure operation here in Hawai'i. This integration serves as a model for the rest of the country and is being replicated here in Hawai'i and the mainland. The Juvenile Detention Facility is particularly noteworthy because it provides a safe environment with educational, recreational, counseling, and medical services before and during hearings in the courthouse. The facility balances safety and monitoring needs within a small-scale, residential environment.

For an emotionally charged environment, providing interior spaces designed to connect and support was vital. Circular ceiling designs evoke the Hawaiian practice, *ho'oponopono*, a traditional dispute resolution approach in which the community participated in a physical circle as means for support through "righting a wrong through group effort."

The key to the project's success was the Working Group, members of the judiciary, including judges and administrators who provided ongoing strategy recommendations and guidance. This group represented all levels and divisions. AHL constructed a detailed, life-size courtroom mockup during

Photos: Bad Moon Salon / Max Kim

the schematic design process to allow for easier review and comment by the group who would be using the courtrooms. As a result of their input, the design team made necessary design adjustments.

Early in the design process, the team advocated for the integration of significant and meaningful public art. The inclusion of public art reinforces personal connections between the institution, the citizens of Hawai'i, and the project's specific location on O'ahu. The State Foundation for Culture and the Arts, through collaboration, commissioned two substantial significant public art creations and incorporated many pieces from the State's collection into the building.

Local artist Doug Young, selected to design the five multi-story windows, spent hours at nearby Anianikū Beach, watching the patterns of the water for translation into his creation of dramatic stained-glass windows. The mesmerizing work helped fulfill the goal of providing profound sense of serenity amid the stressful courthouse activity as light plays a vital role in diffusing emotions. In the words of the client, the design achieved "a bright line between transparency and confidentiality" because the art glass shields the view of the family courtroom from public waiting areas.

Local sculptor, Leland Miyano, was commissioned to provide the impressive stone pieces in the courtyard. His two sculptures reflect the dualistic nature of Hawaiian cosmology. The physical distance between the two suggests a metaphorical and metaphysical journey, and the stones reveal their volcanic heart and imply both water and island forms. Miyano's pieces anchor the community to its voyaging past.

To make the Judiciary Complex more sustainable, the design took advantage of abundant natural light and used recycled and local-content materials. Additionally, the team applied stormwater management, light pollution reduction, water-efficient landscaping, water-use reduction, low-emitting materials, and thermal comfort monitoring and control to the Complex.

As a significant State facility and center in Kapolei, the Ronald T. Y. Moon Kapolei Judiciary Complex promotes an innovative, compassionate, and culturally respectful image of Hawai'i. •

PROJECT CREDITS

CLIENT
State of Hawai'i, DAGS

ARCHITECT
AHL

INTERIOR DESIGN
AHL

CONTRACTOR
Unlimited Construction Services, Inc.

Photo: Paul Hiffmeyer

AULANI, A DISNEY RESORT AND SPA

COMPLETED

2012

Photo: David Roark

From the very onset of architectural selection to completion of Disney® Aulani's "bricks and mortar" resort, both design and execution focused on expressing Disney's unique brand of storytelling.

Respect and appreciation for Hawai'i's culture and traditions were tantamount. At the same time, designers recognized that the experiential "Disney Difference," which defines Disney's brand throughout the world, needs to be omnipresent throughout the full spectrum of guest experiences.

Walt Disney® Imagineering's team culture is open, collaborative, communicative, and highly engaged with design all around them. AHL's selection for Aulani came through Disney's recognition of shared culture and the capability to deliver large complex projects.

The design process focused on building consensus by having all stakeholders around the table listening, learning, discussing with openness, and then moving forward with conviction. This collaborative culture spread and engaged everyone involved in Aulani's creation; architects and landscape architects, engineers and specialty consultants, contractors and subs, and importantly Ko Olina Resort's ownership and the local community.

Surprise and delight are essential "Disney Difference" ingredients, often achieved by thinking outside the box. AHL's Aulani team engaged seamlessly with Disney® Imagineering from concept through details and execution, jointly executing Aulani's "Disney Vision."

Aulani means "The Place that speaks for the ancestors, the place that speaks with deep messages." Disney Imagineers joined with members of the local community to craft how Aulani's story would unfold for guests. The result was an immersive experience that engages with Hawaiian culture and the land, revealed through storytelling. The works of Hawai'i artists tell many chapters of this story. Aulani is now home to the most extensive collection of Hawaiian art and artifacts outside of Bishop Museum.

As a resort, Aulani comprises 359 hotel rooms and 481 Disney Vacation Club® two-bedroom equivalent timeshare villas in two 16-story towers. Low-rise common indoor and outdoor elements include an 18,000-square foot spa, a 14,500-square-foot conference center, and outdoor venues placed over roughly eight acres throughout the resort property. On-site restaurants feature Hawaiian cuisine in a picturesque setting featuring spectacular sunset views along the famous Leeward Coast. Feature areas include a wedding lawn with a serene view of the Pacific, a Disney Kids' Club with custom-planned activities

Photo: Paul Hiffmeyer

WALT DISNEY IMAGINEERING'S TEAM CULTURE IS OPEN, COLLABORATIVE, COMMUNICATIVE, AND HIGHLY ENGAGED WITH DESIGN ALL AROUND THEM.

Photo: Paul Hiffmeyer

Photo: David Roark

Photo: Bad Moon Salon / Max Kim

and adventures, and a signature waterway at the pool that weaves through volcanic rockwork. More adventurous family members can swim with vibrant tropical fish in a saltwater snorkel lagoon.

The plan called for extensive fill on Aulani's mostly level site to create a stunning above-grade entry arrival experience with lobby views down to the ocean. The Hawaiian Ahupua'a philosophy was adopted for Aulani, expressing Hawai'i environments "from the mountain to the sea." Lush landscaping abounds at the *mauka* (mountain) portion of the site, transitioning to more open areas with stands of coconut palms punctuating the *makai* (ocean) side site, culminating with a dramatic volcanic caldera.

The towers emphasize Hawaiian design elements, including *kapa* (Hawaiian bark cloth) motifs, vertical bound bamboo, and thatch "canoe-house"-style roofs. The buildings are integrated into the site's decorative rockwork, pools, other water-related features, and subtle Hawaiian myth symbology.

Multiple dining experiences range from casual beachside snacks and shave ice to oceanfront open-air fine dining. Special effects and creative lighting add to the unique atmosphere during the day and through the evening. Experiencing Aulani is immersive, fun-filled, culturally rich, and memorable to everyone, everywhere. •

PROJECT CREDITS

CLIENT
Walt Disney Imagineering

ARCHITECT
AHL

DESIGN AND VISION
Walt Disney Imagineering in collaboration with WATG

INTERIOR DESIGN
AHL, Walt Disney Imagineering, KNA Interior Design

CONTRACTOR
Hawaiian Dredging Construction Company

DESIGN PRINCIPLES

- Incorporate Hawaiian arts, architecture, patterns, colors, and materials
- Optimize ocean-view rooms
- Maximize oceanfront garden space to accommodate recreational activities
- Provide a view corridor through the center of the site
- Building layout to meet phasing strategy

AHL OFFICE

Photo: Bad Moon Saloon / Max Kim

COMPLETED **2012**

From the first office in 1946 at AHL's founder's garage in Waikīkī, AHL's work environment has long been at the core of the firm's ethos. While that original workspace could not afford the luxury of a truly designed setting, it was a critical initial step for a small group of design pioneers to establish their vision for creating modern architecture in Hawai'i's tropical environment.

Hawai'i's transition from a remote territory to a new State of the Union in 1959 propelled the young firm's rapid growth. In just 13 years, AHL had become a design firm of stature with significant commissions, including the Hawai'i State Capitol. By 1959 AHL's work environment was not only designed but located in its largest project, on the 15th floor of Hawai'i's newest and tallest building, the 17-story First Hawaiian Bank Tower. By then, the firm had developed a pattern of designing its offices in one of its projects. This tradition continues to this day with AHL's current office in the Pacific Guardian Center (PGC), designed by the firm in the early 1980s.

AHL envisioned each of its five major locational moves as opportunities to rethink how the studio environment can stimulate and support the design process. From that initial garage to today's 31st Floor PGC, open spaces where people gather, discuss, and create have been the physical expression of AHL's collaborative design culture. From the 1980s on, technology

Photos: Bad Moon Saloon / Max Kim

accelerated the transition from spacious individual work areas with fixed meeting rooms and paper drawings; to computer technology, simultaneously enabling digital design creation and instant collaborative communication from a variety of environments and locations.

The most notable change took place when AHL moved into its current PGC officespace at the end of 2012. Drafting boards became a thing of the past, and individual personal space shrank to just seven linear feet per person. Private offices had already disappeared in the previous ASB Tower location, with principals and staff in open workstations. The new office partitions were lowered providing visual connectivity and natural light and views throughout the space. Meetings take place at workstations, in casual seating groups, and in small rooms with operable glass partitions called *hokus* (star). The flexible space plan allows for sitting, standing, and movable conference tables, with attendees joining in person or remote. Large monitors abound, including walls, which become desktops. People attend meetings in person, on Zoom, Microsoft Teams, and other applications, using laptops and cell phones. The 3D laser printer creates study models replacing hand-cut cardboard. Regardless of how or where design teams work, staff can quickly view and respond to the design in 2D and 3D.

Designed to be LEED Silver, the office features a large *'ohana* (community) room that can accommodate the whole office for events, full kitchen, shower, sleep room, and recycling program. The office environment utilized abundant natural daylighting, energy-efficient task lighting, low-flow water fixtures, and eco-friendly finishes and materials.

This style of working has been in place since the end of 2012, and AHL's transition to address COVID-19 has been rapid and seamless. At the writing of this book, the firm has been able to work fully-remote for two years in large thanks to the digital infrastructure put in place over the years. AHL is planning how to once again, to improve the office environment as the nature of design work yet again evolves. As always in the firm's history, the professional process evolves jointly with personal and lifestyle goals. AHL's passion for design remains constant, how it is done remains a continuous work in progress. •

PROJECT CREDITS

CLIENT/OWNER
AHL

ARCHITECT
AHL

INTERIOR DESIGN
AHL

CONTRACTOR
J. Kadowaki, Inc.

UNIVERSITY OF HAWAI'I

LIBRARY AND LEARNING CENTER

Photo: Bad Moon Saloon / Max Kim

COMPLETED **2012**

With magnificent views of both the Ko'olau Mountains and Kāne'ohe Bay, Windward Community College (WCC) was established on the site of the old Territorial Hospital in 1972.

The design of the new campus buildings have carried forward the Territorial Hospital's Spanish Mission revival legacy in a natural rural environment. WCC's strengths are Hawaiian studies, natural sciences, fine arts, veterinary technology, and vocational training. Essential campus facilities include Palikū Theatre; Hōkūlani Imaginarium (a full-dome planetarium); Aerospace Exploration Lab physical science exploratorium; Lanihuli Observatory; Gallery 'Iolani; and the new Library/Learning Resource Center, which opened in 2012.

AHL used an integrated design process, enabling students, teachers, and administrators to establish the design program and direction. Discussions included studies showing that since natural light is critical to learning, windows and skylights should provide the majority of light.

AHL's resultant design concept provided open common areas on each of three floors, connected by an atrium with large window walls bringing natural daylight in and beautiful views out. A pedestrian mall level features colonnaded walkways, low massing with Spanish tiled roofs, shaded lanai, and generous landscaping. The main floor spaces include information commons; study rooms; tutoring services; labs for math, speech, and writing; and a coffee shop. Spaces on the Lower Floor include periodicals lounge, computer classroom, study areas, media instruction, and tech support.

In recognition of WCC's history and culture, the design of the 65,000-square-foot Library expresses a blending of campus Spanish Mission revival massing and forms together with modern materials, details, and systems. The College utilizes the building as a campus academic center and gathering place. In scale with surrounding campus structures and integrated with the

Photo: Bad Moon Saloon / Max Kim

beauty of the Ko'olau Mountain Range, WCC's Library Learning Commons fosters student interaction and life-long learning.

The Windward Community College Library/Learning Center achieved LEED Silver designation and is the first LEED-certified library in the University of Hawai'i system. •

AWARDS

- AIA Honolulu People's Choice Award (2014)
- Building Industry Association, Renaissance Overall Grand Award for New Commercial (2014)
- Building Industry Association, Renaissance Grand Award, Hawaii BuiltGreen™ Division, National Green Standard Commercial (2014)
- American School & University Architectural Portfolio, Outstanding Designs and Citation Winner (2014)
- American School & University Educational Interiors Showcase, Outstanding Designs and Citation Winner (2014)
- LEED Certified Silver, U.S. Green Building Council (2014)
- Masonry Institute of Hawaii, Project of the Year (2011)
- AIA Honolulu People's Choice Award
- Building Industry Association, Renaissance Overall Grand Award for New Commercial
- Building Industry Association, Renaissance Grand Award, Hawaii BuiltGreen Division, National Green Standard Commercial
- American School & University Educational Interiors showcase, Outstanding Designs and Citation Winner
- Masonry Institute of Hawaii, Project of the Year
- American School & University Architectural Portfolio, Outstanding Designs and Citation Winner
- LEED Silver, U.S. Green Building Council

PROJECT CREDITS

CLIENT
University of Hawai'i

ARCHITECT
AHL

INTERIOR DESIGN
AHL

CONTRACTOR
Absher Construction Company

FBI HONOLULU FIELD OFFICE

COMPLETED **2012**

The Federal Bureau of Investigation's new Kapolei Field Office was envisioned as a modern and sustainable gateway to the Kalaeloa District.

General Services Administration based the selection for this design-develop-build-leaseback project on the overall quality of aesthetic design, performance criteria specifications, functionality, gross area, cost, and schedule. AHL's winning team's proposal required intense and ongoing interaction and collaboration between all entities from design inception through construction and turn-over.

The four-story, 152,000-square-foot structure includes a 20,000-square-foot annex for automotive and electronic repairs plus secure parking for 350 vehicles. The facility provides for the hundreds of FBI agents, analysts, task force officers, and other support personnel protecting the Hawai'i region.

The Hawai'i Community Development Authority envisioned the field office serving as a modern gateway to the Kalaeloa District, while honoring its historic and cultural roots. AHL's design approach focused on the creation of a building with a civic presence that relates to Hawai'i's overall community while addressing the FBI's non-stop operational requirements. Exterior precast panels use integral color and feature culturally-inspired weaving patterns, common in traditional Hawaiian culture. Large areas of glass on the façade lighten the building presence and provide expansive views from Diamond Head to the Wai'anae Mountains while also providing ample natural daylighting. The glass both meets energy requirements and, in conjunction with concrete wall panels, provides the blast and energy performance levels necessary for this high-performance facility.

This LEED Gold Certified complex, with its innovative and sustainable green design features, embodies and exceeds the goals of the General Services Association's Design Excellence Program, as well as the Hawai'i 2050 Sustainability Plan. Expressing Hawai'i's intrinsic intertwining of environmental and cultural sustainability, weaving patterns were additionally

Photo: Bad Moon Saloon / Max Kim

integrated into the interior design and the exterior spandrels panels. They symbolize the FBI's commitment to *'ohana* (community), which it protects and serves. Vine motifs also on spandrels express the Hawaiian theme of *kolokolo,* representing investigation and moving smoothly with humility. The FBI's highly functional and efficient Kapolei Field Office is a valuable and sustainable member of the community, serving and protecting, with respect. •

PROJECT CREDITS

CLIENT
Penrose / Walsh FBI Honolulu, LLC

ARCHITECT
AHL

INTERIOR DESIGN
AHL

CONTRACTOR
Archer Western / Charles Pankow Builders Joint Venture

CAMP SMITH SEMPER FIT CENTER

COMPLETED **2014**

AHL's Camp Smith Fitness Center is an important addition to one of Hawai'i's most significant United States Military installations.

A US Marine Corps installation in the Hawaiian town of 'Aiea, on O'ahu, Camp Smith is home of the US Pacific Command (USPACOM), with all US military units located in Hawai'i falling under USPACOM's command. Camp Smith is unique as it is the only Marine Corps installation that supports a unified Commander, Indo-Pacific Command (CDRUSINDOPACOM).

Camp Smith's hillside 220-acre sugar cane field site was purchased through an Act of Congress on March 17, 1941, for a Navy Hospital. The 1,650-bed facility was rushed to completion following the December 7th Pearl Harbor attack and served thousands of wounded sailors and Marines during WWII. Hospital activity peaked following the battle for Iwo Jima in early 1945, when 5,676 patients received medical care simultaneously. Camp Smith's present command significance first emerged during the 1950s, developing and increasing with ongoing US military organizational improvements to its current high status.

Today's Camp Smith is a robust mixed-use US military environment with a scenic hillside setting, centrally located and convenient to Pearl Harbor and other military installations. Camp Smith provides a pleasant residential environment, yet its secluded and high-security environment makes on-base lifestyle facilities especially important. The new Physical Fitness Center benefits more than 2,500 service members and government and civilian employees and families, replacing the limited exercise capability in the basement of an old hospital wing, which was not meeting the community's need.

Photo: Bad Moon Salon / Max Kim

The 30,000-square-foot Physical Fitness Center is modern and state-of-the-art. Facilities include a fitness area, gymnasium, exercise rooms with showers, locker rooms, administrative offices, and classrooms. Serving as a model fitness center for all Marine Corps and Department of Defense (DoD) installations in Hawai'i and the Pacific Region, AHL's Camp Smith Physical Fitness Center's mission is to promote and maintain morale and efficiency of Marine Corps personnel and their families by promoting physical health and mental well-being.

Design-Build was utilized as Camp Smith Fitness Center's project delivery system, offering the best possible design-and-cost effectiveness balance. Integral with Camp Smith's restrained aesthetic, natural palette, and quiet environment, the center's high ceilings and clerestory windows bathe the fitness spaces in luminous natural light. The predominantly masonry building features a variety of smooth, split-faced, and integrally colored concrete masonry units (CMU), enhancing visual interest through patterns, surface textures, and colors.

Camp Smith Fitness Center's structural design is in accordance with DoD's Anti-Terrorism/Force Protection (ATFP) requirements. Specially designed CMU blocks act both as load-bearing and shear for lateral resistance, including the necessary support for the ATFP loads on windows. In 2013 the Masonry Institute of Hawaii awarded the Camp Smith Semper Fit Center its Project of the Year.

Energy conservation was the Design-Build team's highest priority. The Center incorporates numerous sustainable design features, including energy management, solar light tubes, underground stormwater infiltration chambers, recycled materials, waste management, and photovoltaic panels that offset 100 percent of projected energy demand. Responding to the DoD's strong commitment to a sustainable future, Camp Smith Fitness Center achieved LEED Platinum, exceeding the DoD's LEED Gold standard requirement for the project. •

PROJECT CREDITS

CLIENT
NAVFAC Hawaii

ARCHITECT
AHL

INTERIOR DESIGN
AHL

CONTRACTOR
Nan, Inc.

AWARDS

- GCA of Hawaii Design Build Award, 2015
- NAIOP Kukulu Hale Award, Green Building Award, 2015
- Masonry Institute of Hawai'i, Project of the Year, 2014
- Building Industry Association, Renaissance Grand Award, Hawai'i BuiltGreen™ Division, National Green Standard Commercial, 2014
- LEED Certified Platinum, U.S. Green Building Council, 2014

SYMPHONY HONOLULU

COMPLETED **2016**

Prominently located at Honolulu's high trafficked intersection of Ward Avenue and Kapi'olani Boulevard, Symphony Honolulu was completed in 2016.

The tower comprises a 43-story residential condominium with multi-level parking and a significant retail podium housing Velocity Honolulu, a mixed-use anchor tenant with diversified entertainment venues and a retail auto galleria.

Symphony Honolulu has 385 residences, of which 273 are market rate, with 100 reserved affordable units and 12 penthouses. Also designed by AHL, Velocity was envisioned as a world-class auto galleria presenting 18 brands of exceptional European cars and motorcycles with a fine-dining restaurant, café, men's clothing store, and unisex beauty salon. Symphony's residents enjoy an extensive "Plaza Earth" amenity deck offering a lap pool, spas, fitness center with indoor yoga, locker room and sauna, multimedia room, karaoke room, social room with chef's kitchen, massage therapy, barbeque and party pavilions, showcase grille, guest suites, and a dog run.

Symphony Honolulu's design vision is the product of intensive collaboration with the clients of the tower and luxury car showroom below. An in-depth charette process enabled architects, interior designers, contractors, brokers, engineers, and other specialty consultants to craft a harmonious design narrative to express the clients' missions and brands. The project aspires to be elegant, timeless, and grounded in a uniquely Hawaiian modern style. The design's development focused on establishing project priorities to help keep the project affordable for the local community despite increasing construction costs island-wide.

Photo: Andrea Brizzi
SYMPHONY

Plaza Earth's richly landscaped design provides a seamless integration between indoor and outdoor amenity spaces. Comfortable spaces for small and large groups enhance feelings of community, quality of living, and social interaction. Guest Residents and guests experience the amenity deck through a series of screened landscape, gathering, and open spaces that offer both tranquility and activity.

Symphony Honolulu was the first 400-foot high-rise residential condominium to achieve LEED Certification in the State of Hawai'i and met the State's and HCDA's Green Building requirements. Symphony's central photovoltaic panel installation provides 77,158 kilowatt-hours of renewable energy annually, offsetting common area energy usage and approximately $25,000 of overall electrical fees each year. Highly efficient plumbing fixtures offer over 35 percent total potable water savings within the building. These provisions ensure that Symphony does its part in protecting Hawai'i's water resources for future generations. •

DESIGN PRINCIPLES

1. Floor-to-ceiling glass in all residential tower units, including reserved housing units.
2. Tower east-west orientation for maximum sustainability, reducing heat gain, and increasing energy efficiency.
3. Provision of photovoltaic panels surrounding "Plaza Earth," providing energy savings for residents and the commercial operator.
4. USGBC Silver Certification.
5. Transparent and engaging storefronts activate the pedestrian experience.
6. Façade glazing designed to blend into the sky during sunny and cloudy weather. Engages sky color during all weather and time of day.
7. A "lantern" facade design helps residents and guests find the main residential entrance illuminated evening mode.
8. The landscaped amenity deck, "Plaza Earth," provides a garden experience for all the residents.

PROJECT CREDITS

CLIENT
Oliver McMillan

ARCHITECT
AHL

DESIGN ARCHITECT
Gensler

INTERIOR DESIGN
Philpotts Interiors, Jules Wilson ID

CONTRACTOR
Nordic PCL Construction, INC.

KA MAKANA ALI'I

COMPLETED **2016**

Located in West O'ahu's "Second City" of Kapolei, Ka Makana Ali'i (KMA) is O'ahu's newest and third largest mixed-use center. The 755,000-square-foot Phase One is complete and the future phases will increase the overall development to 1.4 million-square-feet.

Ka Makana Ali'i's origins stem from its land ownership by the State Department of Hawaiian Homelands. DHHL's mission is derived from the Hawaiian kingdom monarchy ceding its lands to provide "betterment of the conditions of the native Hawaiians." Conceived and master-planned in the 1970s and '80s, O'ahu's "Second City" Kapolei grew and prospered. At the time of writing, KMA's ongoing regional growth includes the new University of Hawai'i West O'ahu campus and the pending completion of construction of its vital station on Honolulu's new rail mass transit system.

Recognizing the Kapolei site's strategic retail potential, DHHL initiated a developer selection process for the award of a long-term lease on its property to provide the construction of a regional mixed-use center of significance. Envisioned to serve West O'ahu's communities, lease rent for the 112-acre site would allow DHHL to offer new residential developments for native Hawaiians. DHHL selected DeBartolo Development LLC, bringing its depth of retail design, leasing, and management expertise to the task, and retained AHL for KMA's architect.

Following in-depth interaction with DHHL and the community overall, the project was named *Ka Makana Ali'i* essentially meaning "Gift of the Monarch." AHL set about expressing KMA's meaning in the project design, creating a modern design concept focusing on a quality of life "Gift to the Community."

Photos: Bad Moon Saloon / Max Kim

As the only regional mixed-use center on West O'ahu, KMA provides a vibrant indoor-outdoor retail-lifestyle mix of shopping, dining, entertainment, grocery, healthy living, and social interaction, previously only found many miles away in urban Honolulu. AHL's design concept focused on creating an experiential "Gift" to Kapolei and all West O'ahu communities, offering gathering places in enriched lifestyle environments. A wide range of exterior spaces frame a department store, pet store, supermarket, specialty clothing and footwear, multi-plex theater, fitness center, medical clinic, and a multitude of dine-in and take-out restaurants. KMA's 100 tenants include national brands previously found only in Honolulu's and Waikīkī's premier malls.

KMA's architecture focuses on large outdoor spaces for dining, gathering, and social interaction. Landscaping combines with trellises and canopies to provide shaded and visual screens. Experiencing KMA is about an exciting shopping environment punctuated by artwork, benches, and lawn areas, altogether creating comfort and a modern sense of place unique to Kapolei.

The design of an L-shaped mall plan anchored by a major department store (Macy's) at one end and a dining and entertainment center (multi-plex movie and restaurants) at the other end met the challenges of the site's shape and configuration. The intersection of the "L" features an engaging central space for community gathering and special events. Also anchoring the angle is KMA's 175-room Hampton Inn Hotel, a unique community asset serving West O'ahu's residential and business needs.

The design utilized tilt-up concrete construction to form KMA's architecture. Storefronts activate the eye level in outdoor spaces framed by trellises and shading elements. A fresh modernist style provides a warm, welcome, and distinctive shopping experience. Shadows dramatize in daytime, and from late afternoons through cool evenings, special lighting energizes KMA's series of minimalistic high fashion gathering places.

KMA's unique expression of "Modern Hawaiian Sense of Place" is in clear contrast with other O'ahu retail developments and has been embraced by the West O'ahu Community. •

PROJECT CREDITS

CLIENT
DeBartolo Development

ARCHITECT
AHL

INTERIOR DESIGN
AHL

CONTRACTOR
Nordic PCL Construction

PUNCHBOWL COLUMBARIUM

Photo: Bad Moon Saloon / Max Kim

COMPLETED **2017**

Constructed in 1948, the National Memorial Cemetery of the Pacific (NMCP) serves on the Pacific Region from World War II to the present day and receives over five million visitors yearly.

NMCP joins Arlington, Gettysburg, and 171 other significant military burial places across the country. These national cemeteries, created by Congress during the Civil War, are administered by the National Cemetery Administration of the Department of Veterans Affairs.

Few national cemeteries command such a powerful and picturesque natural setting as the NMCP. The Punchbowl Crater is an extinct volcanic tuff cone that was formed 75,000 to 100,000 years ago due to secondary volcanic activity. The crater resulted from lava ejecting through coral reef cracks, which, at the time, extended to the foot of the Ko'olau Mountains. Punchbowl's Hawaiian name, *Pūowaina* (Hill of Sacrifice) connects the past to the present and serves as a worthy location to honor those men and women who served in the United States Armed Forces, and those who have given their lives in doing so.

The Public Information Center (PIC) rests on steeply sloping Federal land outside the crater, effectively removing vehicular and tour bus activity, which previously detracted from Punchbowl's desired memorial experience. AHL's design goal was to project a dignified, contemporary presence that would not compete with Punchbowl's existing 1940s art deco design character and formal environment. The PIC welcomes and orients visitors and houses administrative staff as well as the honor guard that accompanies funeral corteges. The PIC's single-story

Photos: Bad Moon Saloon / Max Kim

entry massing descends into the hillside, complementing the surrounding neighborhoods. Views from the PIC look out towards Diamond Head and surrounding hills.

The PIC's floor plans and resultant massing consist of three main sections angled to reduce scale and nestle the structure into the hillside. The low profile "butterfly roof" breaks the form down, creating varied views toward Diamond Head from PIC vantage points. The unique roof dramatizes the stunning views and brings eastern daylight into the LEED Silver building. Built into the slope, the PIC maintains a low profile both from the residential side and the valley below. Darker finishes on its downhill side blend in with the sloping hillside environment. At the same time, a lighter travertine stone on the entry façade establishes a quiet public presence within the residential neighborhood. Maintaining non-intrusive views of Punchbowl from surrounding areas was a high priority.

The steeply sloping site on the side of Puowaina Crater included undocumented soil as it served as a debris depository for the past 50 years. The design called for the removal of existing earth and regrading of the site. Three retaining walls provide a stable base for the building, each over 100 feet long and up to 20 feet high with structure resting on 60 concrete piers, descending 30-feet to volcanic tuff.

Providing serene, private spaces for families to meet with staff was a high design priority. Design execution reflects The US Department of Veterans Affairs' specific programmatic and adjacency requirements while creating spaces appropriate to Hawai'i's unique environment. The Hawaiian legend of the *'Ohi'a Lehua* tree, a story of unconditional love, was used as design inspiration for the building interiors, with accent colors reminiscent of this famous tree used throughout. Natural materials such as stone and wood tie back to Hawai'i's sense of place. •

PROJECT CREDITS

CLIENT
Department of Veterans Affairs, National

ARCHITECT
AHL

INTERIOR DESIGN
AHL

CONTRACTOR
Nan. Inc.

WALGREENS FLAGSHIP STORE

COMPLETED **2017**

Walgreens entrusted AHL as the architect for its new flagship store, and together the team chose the corner of Kapi'olani and Ke'eaumoku for the project site.

Kapi'olani Boulevard and Ke'eaumoku Street is one of Honolulu's most visible and bustling intersections, and some residents refer to it as "the corner of Main & Main." Ala Moana Shopping Center's pivotal main entrance is at this intersection along with one of Honolulu's stations. Lively pedestrian activity and continuous vehicular traffic make this one of the most visible and active locations on O'ahu.

Following the selection of this prominent site, AHL's design team set about creating an architecturally significant and unique landmark rooted in Hawai'i's cultural traditions. A critical project objective was to redefine the Walgreens brand's physical environment and product offerings in the context of Hawai'i's diverse mosaic of people, cultures, and tastes. A related goal was improving and re-energizing the surrounding pedestrian environment by improving site visibility and strategically locating the entry point to create an active urban space on the main corner.

AHL's overall design intent was to create a culturally inspired, publicly relevant, and architecturally significant building to express the Walgreens brand in Hawai'i. The building structure was a modified version of the traditional Hawaiian Hale A-Frame, featuring transparent glass and metal cladding to create an inviting environment for customers and passersby. In Hawaiian, *Ala Moana* means "path to the sea," and the Ala Moana area served as the source of inspiration for the design throughout the building.

> *"We wanted to create a space that would pay homage to Hawaiian culture in a modern, contextually appropriate way."*

said AHL's Director of Design & Sustainability, Lester Ng.

refreshing
olu'olu
Photos: Bad Moon Saloon / Max Kim

pick up express Rx
Welcome

Inspiration for the exterior metal panels motif came from the undulating movement and flow of water from the mountain to the sea. The ground floor used elements and colors representative of the *kai* (sea), with an undulating *nalu* (wave) light fixture connecting the two entrances and unifying the store. A series of wood trellises float near the ceiling, and represent the *'upena* (fishnet) that early Hawaiian fishermen used in the area while the second floor of the store shifted towards earthier tones. The large glass curtain wall offered enticing interior views to all the pedestrians out on the street. Once inside, shoppers' experiences included views of Honolulu's magnificent Ko'olau mountains and streetscape through the veil of Kapiolani's expansive monkeypod canopy trees. Interior features, including custom-designed ceiling elements representing the *ao* (cloud), enhance the volume and scale of the spaces.

Walgreens Flagship Store included a café, smoothie bar, sushi and poke bar, and on-the-go meals, while escalators passed through atrium spaces enhancing views and experiences. The upper level had a pharmacy, private health room, and boutique beauty department.

The Walgreen's Flagship Store received the International Council of Shopping Centers' 2016 ICSC VIVA Retail Store Design Award, which honors projects from around the world that demonstrate vision, innovation, value, and achievement in design, development, sustainability, marketing, and retail. •

PROJECT CREDITS

CLIENT
Walgreens Realty Resources

ARCHITECT
AHL

INTERIOR DESIGN
AHL

CONTRACTOR
DCK Pacific

AWARDS

- ICSC VIVA Award Retail Store Design, 2016
- ICSC US Design and Development Award Competition, Gold Award, 2015
- Building Industry Association, Grand Award for New Commercial Projects more than 15,001 SF, 2015
- GCA of Hawaii, Excellence Award for Design Assist/ Design Build, 2016
- GCA of Hawaii, Grand Award, 2016

KEKU'IAPOIWA LEARNING CENTER

Photo: Bad Moon Saloon / Max Kim

COMPLETED **2017**

The new Kamehameha Schools Keku'iapoiwa Learning Center highlights 21st-century learning by wrapping a priceless cultural history with a vibrant contemporary design.

AHL redesigned the existing 9,400-square-foot Kamehameha Schools High School library from a traditional and reserved research space to a next-generation space where students can share, collaborate, and create. The design inspiration was based on transforming old static library stacks into a social space that supports contemporary learning modalities. A "learning center" is a hybrid, part school, part home, and part coffee-shop, all designed to be active, flexible, and comfortable.

The design team found innovative ways to overcome familiar problems on Hawai'i Island's rain-soaked west side. The school was able to restore damaged shelving and books. Preserved wood tables were encased in laminate to prevent future damage.

The overall design vision transformed the old high school library into a popular student space with fresh energy and attraction. Open, flexible spaces were created by reconfiguring circulation and reference desks in flanking positions. Configurable furniture accommodates a variety of learning and meeting sizes and formats. Designers added pairs of breakout rooms and classrooms, private meeting areas and kiosks, a student-run café, and a "makerspace" for crafts, presentations, and group projects.

Photo: Bad Moon Saloon / Max Kim

AHL's mauka-to-makai motif features a *piko* (navel, center) in the center of the room and sets the scene through color and shapes. Lush green tones dominate the center's mountainside, while cool blues sweep through its oceanside. Gray-colored tiles blanket the middle *piko* space, representing the volcano that birthed the mountains and filled the ocean.

The center of the space also houses a collection of ancient and delicate Hawaiian artifacts. The collection required protective, innovative design elements to prevent sunlight damage, theft, and potential mismanagement, while still being displayed in open, accessible areas. Historic poi pounders are mounted vertically on a wall with specially designed claw-like metal brackets to keep visible and protected. Designers provided a mobile display stand to showcase a traditional canoe, with the stand representing the canoe floating on water.

From its opening, the new Keku'iapoiwa Learning Center resonated with students through its stimulating environment, which provides an immersive Hawaiian cultural, educational experience. It has become a gathering place on the Kamehameha Schools' Hawai'i Campus, a space for the students to grow through sharing knowledge, experience, and perspectives. •

PROJECT CREDITS

CLIENT
Kamehameha Schools

ARCHITECT
AHL

INTERIOR DESIGN
AHL

CONTRACTOR
Isemoto Contracting Co.

VELOCITY HONOLULU

COMPLETED **2018**

Driven by the shared vision to reinvigorate Honolulu, Velocity Honolulu contributes to Live.Work.Play neighborhoods and encourages healthy lifestyles in Transit-Oriented development.

Velocity Honolulu is much more than the average car dealership. A significant part of this development's vision was to encourage each tenant to be part of the greater shared branding of Velocity. This vision put aside individual requirements in favor of a process that embraces the idea that "the whole exceeds the sum of its parts" in crafting a modern, luxurious, multi-functional events and arts space.

Velocity is a creative and entertaining retail anchor tenant in the LEED Certified Symphony Honolulu high-rise mixed-use development, located at Honolulu's visible and high-trafficked crossroads intersection of Ward Avenue and Kapi'olani Boulevard. Housed in the lower portion of Symphony's 70-foot podium, Velocity's three-story transparent glass façade provides interest and excitement to passers-by along both principal thoroughfares. Its glass floor displays unique cars 30-feet above street level and is itself a memorable urban design element. Special lighting effects add delight inside and out during evenings.

The design vision required redefining the "auto dealership" into a museum quality "auto galleria." Fifteen exotic European car and cycle brands combine with niche boutique retail in a minimalistic setting to create an atmosphere that exudes sophisticated design and effortless luxury. As with a museum, the public is encouraged and invited to wander throughout. Trained in five-star hotel customer relations, staff focuses on extolling design and style rather than closing sales. Niche, boutique retail includes a café, auto paraphernalia, specialist clothing, a beauty salon, and fine Italian dining. In addition to sales,

Photo: Andrea Brizzi

the flexible design of Velocity's spaces accommodate multiple receptions, dinners, group meetings, and presentations, which are supported by its café and fine Italian dining restaurant, all of which invite a variety of customers.

These elements, arranged in an intricately winding three-story podium, are interspersed with open wells, balconies, exhibit spaces, and support retail. Openness allows visitors to explore the multi-story Galleria. Automobiles and bikes, furniture and fixtures, graphics and artwork, clothing, food and wine, and a canopy-tree-lined streetscape combine in Velocity's restrained ambiance to create an urban gathering place.

The customer experience extends through valet, dedicated ramps for arrival and pickup, and facility tour, including the unprecedented individual brand maintenance stations within the podium.

AHL's Project Manager, Daniel Moats, is proud of Velocity's versatile nature. "It continues to be an interactive and interesting space, with changing activations," he says.

> *"I also enjoy showing people the auto service floor with its 33 bays, car-washing, and buffing machines. People are always amazed that it exists in this building. I still see different views when I enter the space, which keeps it visually fascinating."* •

PROJECT CREDITS

CLIENT
JN Automotive Group, Inc.

ARCHITECT
AHL

INTERIOR DESIGN
AHL

CONTRACTOR
Unlimited Construction Services, Inc.

LAU HALA SHOPS

Photo: Andrea Brizzi

COMPLETED **2018**

Kailua's magnificent beaches and laid-back lifestyle have long made it one of O'ahu's favorite places to live and visit.

Hawai'i's signature department store chain Liberty House established itself in Kailua following WWII. Its initially modest 1,200-square-foot shop in the fledgling community expanded in 1953 to a 24,000-square-foot store with mezzanine, and again to 66,000-square-feet in 1962. With its extensive products and mid-century modern design, Liberty House was a major retail anchor embraced by Kailua's beachside community. In 2001 Federated Department Stores acquired Liberty House, and the store became Macy's until its closing in 2016.

At that time, Kama'āina firm Alexander & Baldwin (A&B) initiated a master plan to revitalize Kailua's retail core. They engaged AHL to focus on the Liberty House-Macy's building shell as the initial phase.

A&B's vision was to provide multiple tenant spaces of varying sizes, creating an active, eclectic, and pedestrian-focused lifestyle retail experience that resonates with Kailua's community and visitors alike. A&B's development and leasing group and AHL's design team achieved this goal through intense collaboration. Named "Lau Hala Shops," *lau hala* is Hawaiian for the leaves of the hala tree, which historically were and continue to be extensively used for baskets, mats, and hats. The adaptive-reuse design was inspired by the informal beach gathering structures in the area. Natural wood tones were selected to complement the mid-century modern design while making the building more pedestrian in scale. The building's shell preserved the unique brick façade design, and its external scale and masonry structure was softened and embellished with wood screens, soffits, and trellises.

Photos: Andrea Brizzi

Corner restaurants engage with sidewalks through large glass storefronts and outdoor seating. Original Liberty House black iron railing sections with "LH" initials were restored and utilized at the two-story lobby leading to second-floor tenants; the "LH" initials reflect both the history of Liberty House and Lau Hala Shops' name.

Lau Hala Shops received local and national design awards including the 2020 Gold Award in the Renovations and Expansions category in ICSC's annual Global Awards North America.

"We are pleased to share this prestigious award with AHL for the transformation of this iconic building into a gathering place suited for the Kailua community," said A&B EVP, Chief Real Estate Office Lance Parker. "A&B is grateful for the community's input during the design process and for how residents are embracing the Center." •

PROJECT CREDITS

CLIENT
Alexander & Baldwin

ARCHITECT
AHL

CONTRACTOR
Armstrong Builders, LLC

AWARDS

› NAIOP Hawai'i Kukulu Hale Award, 2020

› ICSC North America Design & Development Gold Award, 2020

› Building Industry Association Grand Award, Landscaping Commerical, 2018

AE'O AT WARD VILLAGE

Photo: Andrea Brizzi

COMPLETED **2018**

Located in Honolulu's Kaka'ako area east of Downtown, Ae'o's concept exemplifies the Ward Village urban neighborhood lifestyle. The residential tower, completed in 2018, looms over a six-story parking and retail podium, soaring to Ward Village's 400-foot height limit.

AHL served as the executive architect for Ae'o, teaming with design architects Bohlin Cywinski Jackson. Named after the native Hawaiian Stilt bird that is prevalent in the area, the slanted columns at key entry locations are a design feature that reflects the Ae'o bird's form and movement through the coastal wetlands.

Ae'o's 40-story residential tower is sited *mauka-makai* (mountain to ocean), retaining maximum views towards the ocean from Honolulu's surrounding city areas. Tower apartments feature angled operable windows providing *makai* vistas and high-rise fresh air experiences. The podium, clad with patterned, perforated metal screening featuring artistic abstraction, simulates movement and nature akin to Hawai'i's tradewinds. The stylish rooftop terrace features a dramatic canopy form, framing 360-degree views for residents to enjoy. The tower's overall style, glass façade, and angular geometry combines with the podium's metal screening to provide visual contrast and interest from all directions and distances.

The residential tower houses 466 apartments in 37 different unit types. With a smaller average unit size than most neighboring buildings, Ae'o provides greater affordability and diversity for the Ward Village community overall. Innovative detail design combines small apartment spaces with high energy

Photos: Andrea Brizzi

shared amenities at the podium level. The seventh-floor amenity deck runs *'Ewa* to Diamond Head or west to east, with multiple pools, fitness center and spa, private dining and multi-media rooms, outdoor cabanas, children's play area, and a dog park.

Ae'o's overall design integrates residences and the flagship anchor tenant, Whole Foods Market, through direct, internal apartment-to-market paths, precluding the need to leave the building to access the other. Vehicular access and parking are zoned separately for residences, Whole Foods, project loading and service, and Ward Village customers and visitors overall. Utilizing ramps of innovative double helix configuration with separate entry points from Queen and Halekauwila Streets resulted in the efficient vehicular circulation pattern.

Whole Foods Market at Ae'o, housed in an unprecedented 72,000-square-foot shell, was uniquely conceived. Large, communal venues include restaurants and bars, outdoor balconies, plaza-level seating, and a wide range of pre-cooked specialty and traditional food market offerings.

Overall, Ae'o's combined private and public living spaces enable richly satisfying lifestyles for residents. Achieving LEED Silver Certification, Ae'o exemplifies a culture of living by preserving and respecting Hawai'i's environment. •

PROJECT CREDITS

CLIENT
Howard Hughes Corporation

ARCHITECT
AHL

DESIGNER OF RECORD
Bohlin Cywinski Jackson

CONTRACTOR
Layton Construction

WHOLE FOODS MARKET QUEEN

Photo: Andrea Brizzi

COMPLETED **2019**

Whole Foods Market Queen, the anchor tenant for Ae'o high-rise mixed-use development, is a significant element in Ae'o's overall iconic presence in Honolulu's Kaka'ako Live.Work.Play urban environment.

Whole Foods' flagship store for Hawai'i, Whole Foods Market Queen's highly visible corner presence brings fresh energy to Ward Village's growing retail environment. The market supports the development's focus on relaxed and unique shopping and dining for Honolulu's overall community and is an integral part of daily life for Ward Village residents. From the date of opening, this location became Whole Foods' most successful unit in its Southern Pacific sales region.

Whole Foods Queen's environment uniquely combines grocery shopping, specialty takeout, sit-down dining and bar service, and welcoming lounge spaces. Its 72,000-square-foot, two-level area maintains the Whole Foods Market branding and standards, while paying homage to the island's community, culture, local delicacies, and native beauty. The design concept focuses on providing seamless indoor to outdoor transitions. Form, texture, unexpected scale transitions, and playful use of volume all utilize Hawai'i's intense light and shadow. Together, these elements express the confluence of natural (water, earth, sky) and human-made (shelter, culture, art) elements. Steel and concrete are purposefully left raw and unfinished as a practical take on sustainability,

Photos: Bad Moon Saloon / Max Kim

reflecting the ethos of healthy and organic products. The simple "loft" quality emphasizes the vivid graphics and natural decor that is a prominent part of the Whole Foods brand.

The design of the market's dramatic two-story, double-height glass façade maximizes daylighting and reduces interior lighting. The store's vertical circulation also takes advantage of abundant natural daylight which is unique in supermarket design. The grand staircase, along with the dining and bar areas, is situated near glazing, activating the pedestrian experience on the sidewalk below. The sweeping canopy over the second-level lanai extends into the building, connecting the streetscape with retail space.

Open space for vendors and pop-up kiosks were designed to enhance the overall shopping experience. As with customers, staff offices and break rooms enjoy clear views of Queen Street and the sales floor. A closed-loop refrigeration system that is only the second one in the country and the first for Whole Foods Market provides increased energy efficiency throughout the store.

Whole Foods Market Queen's overall design approach recognizes the local community of Kaka'ako as alive and dynamic. Hawaiian language defines spaces throughout, embracing Kaka'ako's neighborhood culture. Locally sourced mango wood on staircase handrails, acacia wood in bars, and graphics and colors express Honolulu's mountains and ocean, subtly infusing a sense of place. •

PROJECT CREDITS

CLIENT
Whole Foods Hawaii

ARCHITECT
AHL

INTERIOR DESIGNER
DL English Design Studio

CONTRACTOR
Bogart Construction, Layton Construction

KAPOLEI CLINIC & URGENT CARE

Photo: Andrea Brizzi

COMPLETED **2019**

Modern healthcare is constantly looking for new ways to bring quality care into the community and closer to patients. With its Straub Medical Center–Kapolei Clinic & Urgent Care, Hawai'i Pacific Health is doing just that.

Conveniently located in O'ahu's newest shopping center, Ka Makana Ali'i, Hawai'i Pacific Health's largest and most comprehensive clinic in West O'ahu spans 16,000-square-feet over two stories. Services provided include urgent and primary care for adults and children, pediatric sports medicine, obstetrics/gynecology, imaging, laboratory, and specialists.

Successful healthcare services must fit into the busy, everyday lives of the patients, so creating an accessible, efficient, and patient-centric experience was essential. The Team-Based Care Design model developed broke typical healthcare design paradigms with a mix of hospitality and healthcare intended to reduce stress and create serenity for the patients, families, and staff, while maintaining efficiency, cleanliness, and durability. Biophilic design elements connect people to nature, and surface textures impart depth, interest, and wayfinding.

Centralized physician workstations provide direct lines of sight to all patient rooms and facilitate increased collaboration and employee flexibility. Exam rooms are sized and designed to maximize future functionality. Flexible, comfortable, and ergonomic furniture, arranged in a triangular configuration, facilitates conversation between providers and patients.

Creating privacy and working within the existing infrastructure were the primary design challenges. Existing exterior windows provide daylight to the center of the clinic. This natural lighting delivers a modernized approach to

Photos: Andrea Brizzi

energy cost reduction with privacy in mind. To accomplish visual and acoustic privacy while maintaining the "lightness," designers crafted alcoves in the millwork on the exterior side of care team areas. A floating ceiling with high performing ceiling tiles mitigates noise and increases the sense of openness in the space.

A two-story entry lobby balances beauty and practicality. Large second-floor windows fill the entrance with natural daylight while an elegant staircase contributes to simplified wayfinding. The stair location and design promote an active, walkable lifestyle for employees and patients. Warm wooden screens and natural tones accent a clean, neutral interior palette.

Illuminated discs arranged in a "bubble"-inspired composition create a calm and soothing setting in the urgent care waiting area. Decorative windows with backlit resin panels display an image of a nearby beach to strengthen holistic healing.

As a high-traffic healthcare facility, durable and low-maintenance finishes are required and were selected. The base architectural finishes feature a neutral color palette, with flourishes of color added to the furniture finishes and artwork. These finishes provide a cost-effective and easily maintainable solution.

The modern design emphasized rectilinear silhouettes and natural materials. Designers produced a fresh look to complement the growing Kapolei community. They used Straub's branding colors, blue and green, to evoke a sense of coolness and tranquility in West O'ahu's hot and dry environment. •

PROJECT CREDITS

CLIENT
Hawai'i Pacific Health

ARCHITECT
AHL

INTERIOR DESIGN
AHL

CONTRACTOR
Nordic PCL

AWARDS

- Building Industry and Construction Award for Details-Commercial, 2020
- IIDA Ho'ohuli Award, 2019

Photo: Andrea Brizzi
KEAHUOLŪ COURTHOUSE

KEAHUOLŪ COURTHOUSE

COMPLETED

2019

Photo: Andrea Brizzi

A GUIDING PRINCIPLE WAS TO INTEGRATE THIS SIGNIFICANT PUBLIC BUILDING INTO THE LANDSCAPE, COMMUNITY, AND CULTURAL HERITAGE OF WEST HAWAI‘I.

Photo: Andrea Brizzi

The Keahuolū Courthouse was designed to serve and celebrate the people of West O'ahu and give a permanent home to Hawai'i's Third Circuit Court. For more than 30 years the court facilities dotted West Hawai'i in repurposed leased spaces, not initially intended for court functions. They were undersized and lacked adequate security and technology. The result was operational inefficiency and extra cost.

A personal mission for recently retired Hawai'i Chief Judge Ronald Ibarra had long been to bring the court functions together from the three scattered locations. It took more than 25 years to secure the legislative funding, and over six years to complete planning, design, and construction. The project team completed the Keahuolū Courthouse in Kona on time and within budget.

Partnership was essential to making the new courthouse a reality. Through the Department of Land and Natural Resources, the Queen Lili'uokalani Trust generously agreed to allow the State of Hawai'i to acquire the ten acres of land for the new courthouse facility. Dedicated and passionate project teams from the Judiciary and the Department of Accounting and General Services worked tirelessly with the design and construction teams. The State Foundation on Culture and Arts integrated inspiring public art for all who use the courthouse.

"The public will have a full-service facility where they can take care of all court-related matters in a centralized, convenient, and secure environment."

- Third Circuit Chief Judge Greg Nakamura

The first guiding principle for the design was to support the functions of this modern courthouse for all its users. The plan meets the efficiency and security needs of the Court. It expresses the Judiciary's commitment to transparency

and access to justice for all. The three-story 140,000-square-foot facility has five courtrooms, a law library, rooms for grand jurors and regular jurors, offices for Driver's Education, Juvenile and Adult Client Services, Sheriff's operations, and administrative staff. There are 292 parking stalls for court visitors.

The aesthetic design is in order not to distract from the business of the Court. Sara Belczak, Senior Interior Designer, states,

> *"The judges for the new family courthouse in Kona told us they wanted people to recognize the authority of the Court and behave themselves accordingly, in what are often highly charged emotional situations. Our design had to be strong enough to command respectful behavior, but also be open, warm, and reflective of Kona's community and culture."*

The organization of the court functions is clear and direct, making it easy for visitors and users to find the services they need. The wood-clad lobby entrance frames the path towards the Judiciary's services. The well-lit lowered-ceiling area announces the location of the transaction windows, allowing visitors to find their way easily. Natural light at the ends of the corridors guide visitors towards the courtrooms, where they find clearly demarcated wood portals.

The quality of the interior environment eases stress, communicates formality, and enhances productivity. The interior's *ola* color palette uses a variety of dynamic green tones that revitalize and refresh. *ola* means life, health, and well-being. Lowered ceilings in the waiting areas opposite the courtrooms create spaces of comfort and privacy. Natural light in each courtroom, introduced through translucent windows above the bench, helps calm people in the Court and maintain connections to the day outside.

The second guiding principle was to integrate this significant public building into the landscape, community, and cultural heritage of West Hawai'i.

The people of West Hawai'i value the beauty and power of the *'aina* of Keahuolū and prefer buildings that respect this landscape. But a courthouse is by function a significant facility with formal columns and judicial seals used to announce that this building is a State Courthouse. The colonnade directs the visitor to the main entry, and recalls the forms of the traditional American courthouse. At the same time, the architectural and landscape design brings together discrete building elements, as if the courthouse were a collection of smaller buildings. The texture and dark gray color of the building's first floor complements the dark gray *'a'ā* lava of the site, visually reducing the apparent height of the building. The silhouettes of Hualālai, Mauna Kea, and Mauna Loa above the site inspired the undulating profile of the roof.

Ke Kānāwai Māmalahoe, or the Law of the Splintered Paddle, enacted by King Kamehameha I, was the first written law of the Kingdom of Hawai'i; it remains in the State Constitution to this day. Born of an encounter with an innocent fisherman in Puna, Hawai'i, the Law of the Splintered Paddle proclaimed that all innocent people be able to sleep safely on the side of the road unharmed. Graphic designs on the entry columns and interior windows recall this legal heritage and express the Judiciary's commitment to fairness for all.

The State Foundation on Culture and the Arts commissioned site-specific public art that inspires reflection about the *'aina* and community of West Hawai'i. "Creating Kama'āina" by Matt Salenger explores our connection to place. In ancient Hawaiian culture, as a way of connecting a newborn child to the land, the parents buried the child's umbilical cord (*piko* in Hawaiian) in a small crater carved into the ground. The term *kama'āina* means "child of the land," speaking to the deep connection between the Hawaiian people and their land. The figures of "Ho'o Pōhaku" by Jerry Vasconcellos are an affirmation to stand firm in the light of our truths, using stone from Kailua-Kona's beloved Hualālai. The Queen Lili'uokalani Trust graciously endowed on-site studio space at the base of the Keahuolu Courthouse construction site. In a true testament to regenerative cycles and interconnectivity innate to the Hawaiian Islands, the *pohaku* essentially never left their home. •

PROJECT CREDITS

CLIENT
State of Hawai'i Judiciary

ARCHITECT
AHL

INTERIOR DESIGN
AHL

CONTRACTOR
Nan, Inc.

DESIGN PRINCIPLES

- Modern, functional, safe, and secure courthouse
- Integrate landscape, community, and cultural heritage of West O'ahu
- Sustainable design and biophillic interiors

AWARDS

- Building Industry and Construction Award for New Commercial, 2020

SHERATON MAUI RESORT & SPA

Photo: Andrea Brizzi

COMPLETED **2019**

The Sheraton Maui Resort & Spa is blessed to have one of the most magnificent sites in Hawai'i, and one of the most culturally significant natural features—*Pu'u Keka'a* (Black Rock)—on Maui.

Inspired by the dramatic and historic site, the renovation of the 508 guestrooms, suites, and public spaces at the Sheraton Maui Resort & Spa reflects the natural beauty and cultural significance of its location at Pu'u Keka'a while providing the guest a seamless experience between all areas of the resort.

AHL worked with cultural practitioners, and their design process began with the team's immersion into the history, culture, and environmental elements of the site. For the Sheraton Maui Resort & Spa, its storied location made this process particularly important. The client was fully engaged in this process and always desired that the renovations demonstrate a culturally relevant design.

The team researched and found inspiration from the *mo'olelo* (stories and legends) of the island's creation and the *ali'i* (chiefs). Accounts from former residents were shared with the team and provided the foundation for a design narrative steeped in reverence for the cultural history and the natural environment.

The crystal clear waters at Keka'a are ethereal, appearing light turquoise near the shore, then dissolving into shades of sapphire toward the deeper channels. The black rock at Pu'u Keka'a cuts a sharp silhouette against the blue of the ocean and the sand of the beach. This setting, together with the rich cultural narrative, moved the team to highlight contrast and duality, through the curated use of materials, colors, and clean, modern design forms set against the idyllic seascape.

Another unique feature that influenced the overall design concept is the site's relationship to the neighboring islands of Lāna'i and Moloka'i.

Photos: Andrea Brizzi

There is a visual connection between these islands that is found nowhere else in the island chain, and the color palettes used in the hotel's towers reflect their individual island views. The beach at Kā'anapali, at the foot of Pu'u Keka'a, faces towards the cloud-enshrined island of Lāna'i. The Lahaina and 'Ohana tower rooms, which face Lāna'i, are bathed in luminous whites, orange hues, and light wood-grain tones.

The Moana tower has a direct view across the channel to the steep green cliffs of Moloka'i. For these rooms, rich greens and blues with darker wood grains mirror the cerulean channel and the verdant landscape of Moloka'i.

Anchored to Pu'u Keka'a itself are the Nalu and Ānuenue towers, and many of their rooms feature views inland to the West Maui mountains. Here, the design tells the stories of the Maui chiefs in pinks and reds associated with the *ali'i* and the rainbows of the valleys.

Local cultural practitioners and artists developed the corridor wall coverings. The art for the wall covering is inspired by *lewa lani* (layers of the horizon), which are clearly observed from all vantage points of the resort, overlayed with coral from the waters of Kā'anapali.

The Sheraton's lobby was significantly opened to allow for increased daylight and natural ventilation, taking advantage of the Kā'anapali climate and trade winds. Views of the pristine beachfront and the spectacular sunsets were enhanced, offering guests a seamless connection from the lobby lounge to the ocean. Adaptive reuse of previously underutilized spaces provides bespoke food and beverage moments and entertainment for guests. Local artists, curated color palettes, and island-inspired motifs are featured throughout the resort and immerse guests in an environmentally and culturally sustainable island experience. Integral to the design is the story of Chief Kahekili, who would dive from the famous Pu'u Keka'a fronting the resort into the sea to both demonstrate his power and authority as chief, but also to renew himself in the healing waters.

Lisa Rapp, AIA, LEED AP, principal at AHL, explains the sequence crafted for guests as they arrive at the Sheraton Maui Resort:

> *"Pu'u Keka'a is iconic. It tells a story of transition from the physical to the spiritual, and we use that narrative as part of the guest's arrival experience. We want them to shed the burdens of travel, relax, and begin their renewal."* •

PROJECT CREDITS

CLIENT
Kyo-Ya Hotels, LLC

ARCHITECT
AHL

INTERIOR DESIGN
AHL

CONTRACTOR
Swinerton Builders

FEATURED IN

- Architecture & Design *"Design Excellence: Hawaii,"* November 2021

LAND

SEA

SHELTER

CULTURE

AHL and a story of modern architecture in Hawai'i.

ahl.

CREDITS

› TEAM

Raynette Aggabao
Elvin Ashley Agustin
Emile Alano
Carmela Arcenas
Ed Ryan Balbuena
RM Balintona
Sharla Batocal
Thomas Baty
Sara Belczak
William Brizee
David Cerame
Huiyi Chen
Douglas Cheung
Christopher Cobb
Louie Dela Cruz
Michael Ellis
Deirdre Espiritu
Daniel Fabisiak
Dewi Fukuoka
Daniel Funakoshi
Joel Ganotisi
Christopher Gaydosh
Emmanuel Geyrozaga
Crystal Gray
Odette Guillermo
Carolyn Haley
Michael Harrison
Frederick Hong
Michael Honyak
Garret Horimoto
Stephanie Ing
Brad Inovejas
Sean Ishida
Aline Ishii
Arynn Ishikawa
Matthew Isono
Keane Kakuda
Lukas Kaplan
Rachel Kaya
Catherine Kenjo
Michael Kim
Sona Kremitovska
Ryan Lambert
Colette Lee
Jeffrey Lee
Rafael Lee
Jia Ming Li
Linda Lileikis
Sara Livengood
Matthew Loudermilk
Jean-Louis Loveridge
W. Terry McFarland
Bettina Mehnert
Shelby Mendes
Myles Michibata
Jenna Miller
Daniel Moats
Mariel Moriwake
Michael Muronaka
Lester Ng
Charles Nishimoto
Neu-Wa O'Neill
Pamela O'Neill
Raymond Okamoto
Alan Paden
Marc Austin Pader
Teri Patton
Lisa Rapp
Jagjit Riyait
Nathan Saint Clare
Henry Schneider IV
Theodore Shepard
Siraj Sheriff
Keith Snyder
Deirdre Stearns
Katie Stephens
Vince Tamura
Sandee Tanaka
Ronald Tapat
Ethan J. Twer
Michael Unnerstall
Hisako Uriu
Samuel Ustare
Jennifer Wakazuru-Kim
Arthur Watrous Jr.
Andre Weatherford
Sarah West
Abby Wisco
Gigi Wong
Ina Wong
Ryan Yamamoto

› BOOK CONTRIBUTORS

Austin Chun
Crystal Gray
Carolyn Haley
Rachel Kaya
Rafael Lee
Tammy Lee
Bettina Mehnert
David Miller
Nathan Saint Clare
Katie Stephens

› DESIGN AND ARTWORK

Middle Management